D1320162

Let's Hear
JACK HYLES

Burning Messages for the Saved and Unsaved

By Dr. Jack Hyles, Pastor
First Baptist Church, Hammond, Indiana

$2.75

Sword of the Lord Publishers
Murfreesboro, Tennessee

Let's Hear Jack Hyles

SWORD OF THE LORD PUBLISHERS
Murfreesboro, Tennessee

Printed in the United States of America

Introduction

I count it a real joy and privilege to write a brief word of introduction concerning this book of sermons by my good friend, Dr. Jack Hyles.

This man has had a unique and fruitful ministry. He built a great church in Garland, Texas, and his dynamic, soul-winning ministry at the First Baptist Church of Hammond, Indiana, has stirred the entire Chicago area.

These sermons when preached have been used of God in a marvelous way. They have been used to bring many to a saving knowledge of the Lord Jesus; they have caused many a backslidden Christian to return to the Lord; they have caused many a preacher to take fresh courage and preach with greater boldness the unsearchable riches of the Gospel of the grace of God.

There are few greater compliments that I can pay any minister than to say he is a great preacher, but I can say one thing better concerning Jack Hyles, and that is, he is a great soul winner.

May these messages reproduced on the printed page continue to be blessed and used of the Lord.

G. Beauchamp Vick
Temple Baptist Church
Detroit, Michigan

Preface

Here are included two kinds of sermons, representing the remarkably useful ministry of Dr. Jack Hyles. Some of the sermons are to Christians, taken down in great conferences on revival and soul winning. In such conferences thousands of preachers, with many other Christian workers, hear this anointed man of God. These conferences on revival and soul winning were promoted by THE SWORD OF THE LORD and hence this magazine and this editor are sometimes mentioned. The messages were given over a period of years.

Other sermons represent the amazing soul-winning ministry of Dr. Hyles in his present pastorate, the First Baptist Church of Hammond, Indiana, where in the past year there has been an average of slightly more than thirty public professions of faith per week and where a tremendous new church auditorium is nearing completion to house the crowds who attend our brother's ministry.

All these sermons have appeared in THE SWORD OF THE LORD with such a blessed response from readers that we rejoice to make them available in permanent book form.

May the dear Lord use them to stir revival fires, to build holy convictions, to promote soul winning and to win the lost.

John R. Rice, Editor
THE SWORD OF THE LORD

Contents

FOR THE SAVED

FOR THE UNSAVED

Burning Messages for the Saved

1

Digging God's Wells

"And Isaac departed thence, and pitched his tent in the valley of Gerar, and dwelt there. And Isaac digged again the wells of water, which they had digged in the days of Abraham his father; for the Philistines had stopped them after the death of Abraham: and he called their names after the names by which his father had called them. And Isaac's servants digged in the valley, and found there a well of springing water. And the herdmen of Gerar did strive with Isaac's herdmen, saying, The water is our's: and he called the name of the well Esek; because they strove with him. And they digged another well, and strove for that also: and he called the name of it Sitnah. And he removed from thence, and digged another well; and for that they strove not: and he called the name of it Rehoboth; and he said, For now the Lord hath made room for us, and we shall be fruitful in the land. And he went up from thence to Beer-sheba."--Gen. 26:17-23.

Now to me this is one of the most interesting stories in all of the Bible. The story is a very simple story; it is very primitive. Folks have preached on it through the years, but to me it is so applicable to what we face in our country today.

In the story of Abraham and the Philistines, Abraham was a well digger. He had digged three wells--a well called Beer-lahai-roi; a well called Beer-sheba; and a well called

Rehoboth. These three wells were a symbol of God's power and blessing in the life of Abraham. Abraham had left the wells, and the Philistines had filled them up, the one of Beer-lahai-roi, the one at Beer-sheba, and the one of Rehoboth.

Since his father Abraham had been a well digger, Isaac, too, wanted to dig some wells as a symbol of the blessing of God. But instead of digging again the wells of Beer-lahai-roi and Beer-sheba and Rehoboth, Isaac decided he would build wells of his own, a well called Esek and a well called Sitnah. There was strife between the herdmen of Isaac and those of the land; so Isaac decided rather than using the new wells that he had built, he would go back and redig the wells that his father Abraham had digged years before, wells which the Philistines had filled up in the meantime.

Now that is the same thing that we face tonight spiritually in America. Our fathers have digged some deep wells spiritually for God.

My hobby is reading biography. I read every biography I can get my hands on. I have walked beside Moody in the World's Fair revival in Chicago; have sat beside Jonathan Edwards as he preached the great sermon, "Sinners in the Hands of an Angry God." I have felt the heartbeat of Charles G. Finney as I walked with him in the great campaigns in Rochester and across country; have felt the heartbeat of Billy Sunday as I read his life in many books. I have read the life of Dwight Moody in every book that I can find. I love to read biographies of these great men. These great men, my precious friends, have digged some wells in our country, deep spiritual wells.

Yet today, when the Philistines are filling up those wells with modernism and liberalism and new-everything-ism, we face the job, the task, of redigging these wells that these great men have digged in years gone by.

Dear friends, if we don't dig some wells today, we are in a pretty sad shape in our country. That is why we have conferences such as this. Some of us with our little picks and shovels are trying, by God's grace, to redig the wells of Sunday, Moody, Edwards and Spurgeon. And those of us who have read their lives and walked with them and followed them, know a little about what God has done, and what they did for God as they dug the wells deep in our country of old-fashioned revival, evangelism, the power of God, the breath of Heaven, the anointing of God, the preaching against sin, the exalting Christ, the preaching of the new birth. On these old-fashioned, fundamental, basic doctrines, they digged the wells deeply in days gone by. But the liberals have stopped the wells, the Philistines have stopped the wells.

That is why John Rice and others go up and down the country; that is why a few of us little fellows holler and scream and bellow our heads off. Unless somebody digs some wells, our country is in for a sad day.

We Need to Exalt Preaching

One thing I like about the Sword of the Lord conferences is that they are very basic, they are built on preaching. I love preaching. I love old Hell-fire-and-brimstone preaching. We used to say in Texas, just old window-rattling, shingle-pulling, barn-storming, Hell-fire-and-brimstone preaching. That is the kind I like. That is the only kind there really is.

Down in Winston-Salem in a Sword of the Lord conference we were having testimonies in the dining hall. One dear lady stood up and said, "I am saved and I praise the Lord that I am saved." Everybody was crying--one of those boo-hoo type meetings that you love to get in! She said, "I guess I am the only woman here who was ever saved under my own preaching."

Dr. Rice looked up sort of perplexed; all of us began to look the same way. We didn't know what we were in for. We waited to see. She said this: "When I was a kid we used to have preaching meetings. All the kids would preach. One would preach one day, the other would baptize, the other sang the solo. One day it was my time to preach. I was about six years old. I got up and said, 'If you don't get born again, you little old children, you are going to burn in Hell!' " She said, "All of a sudden I got under conviction under my own preaching! I stopped and gave the invitation. I went back in the back and walked down the aisle and got saved under my own preaching!"

Yes, there is something warm, something thrilling about preaching. I don't know what it is, I don't understand all of it, but a fellow can get up and say a little bit of nothing--I mean just wave his hands, holler, scream, and cry a little bit--and people will say, "Man, isn't it wonderful to be a Christian!"

If we don't return to the old-fashioned preaching of these brethren, we are in for it. You mark my word: our little boys and girls, growing up in our homes tonight, are not going to have a good place to go to church when they get older. I want to do my little bit. If my little boy becomes a preacher--God help that he will--I want him, when he preaches the Gospel of Christ, to have a place to preach. I don't want my little boy to die with his head under a guillotine for preaching the Gospel in our country. I want Daddy to do what he can to make it possible for my boys and girls to grow up in a country where you can have Bible conferences and revival campaigns.

Yesterday I got a call. A man was going from Texas to New York. He said, "I have been in revival campaigns. I was pastoring in an eastern town, but I left. They have a court injunction against me for visiting. I was not allowed to witness and go from door to door in my city."

Now that is not in Africa; that is in America! Our country today is facing a sad situation. Fundamental and conservative and orthodox Christians are facing today what our boys and girls may face in their lives--the guillotine, the rope, the gallows, for what they believe and what they stand for, the things we have taught them. And the reason is that we are raising a bunch of spineless preachers and deacons and workers who don't have the courage of God to stand up and fight the Devil. They are mollycoddling the church members, the deacons are leading the preacher, the WMS president has a hook in the nose of the preacher and is leading him around like a little dog following a kid. We are losing the breath of God because we are losing the prophets of yesterday--men who walked with God and knew God. God help us to dig some wells. God help us to dig the wells again that our fathers had digged.

Notice three of these wells if you will, the three Abraham dug. First, the well known as Beer-lahai-roi. Now the word Beer-lahai-roi means God lives and sees things. Second, the well of Beer-sheba, which means the promises of God. Third, the well of Rehoboth, which means fruitfulness or fruit bearing.

I. THE WELL OF BEER-LAHAI-ROI--THE GOD WHO LIVES AND SEES WHAT WE DO

He dug the well of Beer-lahai-roi, which means basically that there is a God who lives and sees what we do. Our forefathers dug the well of preaching and teaching that there is a God in Heaven who sees His people; there is a God in Heaven who hates sin; there is a God in Heaven who punishes sin and God looks down upon His people and is not pleased with them. They used to dig the wells of fighting sin and condemning sin, yet in the days since then the Philistines have filled that well.

Great Preachers of the Past Preached Against Sin

When I read the lives of these great men, I say, "What is the difference in Wesley and Jack Hyles? What is the difference in Moody and me? What is the difference in Charles G. Finney and me? What is the difference in Jonathan Edwards and me? What is the difference in old Sam Jones and me? What is the difference in Billy Sunday and me? What did those fellows have that I don't have?" I think I have found a few answers.

In the first place, we today have lost the burden for sin, the condemnation of sin which all those fellows used to preach. I was reading the other day some sermons by John Wesley. You talk about preaching! If that poor fellow today were turned loose in many Methodist churches, he wouldn't have anything left but the steeple, and it would be on its way down! That poor fellow--why I felt like a pussyfooter. I told my staff, "I am going to preach harder. I have been playing around." I am getting meaner! I told my assistant pastor, "There is one thing wrong with me. I am getting too sissy. I am going to get meaner." Since I have gotten meaner, I have gotten happier! I am just going to get mean.

As the old Negro preacher used to say in Texas when he was trying to say God had called him to heal the sick and raise the dead and cast out devils, "God has called me to heal the dead, cast out the sick and raise the Devil." I have just promised God I am going to raise more devil from now on.

Listen to me: with our dance halls full, with the night clubs full, with bootleggers running wild, with naked women on every street corner, with the cigarette industry selling cancery little packages, with the beer bottles rolling on the night club bars, with boys and girls living in sin and the homes for illegitimate mothers are filled with junior high school girls who have to quit school because they are expecting babies--don't you tell me a preacher can't find some sin to preach against, or worldliness. God help us to be alive.

Read John Wesley's diary sometime. It reads approximately like this:

> "Sunday a.m., May 5, preached in St. Anne.
> Was not asked to come back anymore.

"Sunday, May 5, p.m., preached in St. Johns. Deacons said get out and stay out.

"Sunday, May 12, a.m., preached in St. Jude. Can't go back there either.

"Sunday, May 12, p.m., preached in St. George's. Kicked out again.

"Sunday, May 19, a.m., preached in St. somebody else's. Deacons call special meeting, said I couldn't return.

"Sunday, May 19, p.m., preached on the street; kicked off the street.

"Sunday, May 26, a.m., preached in meadow. Chased out of meadow, bull turned loose in the service. (Right, a bull or an ox turned loose in the service.)

"Sunday, June 2, a.m., preached out at the edge of town. Kicked off the highway.

"Sunday, June 2, p.m., afternoon, preached in the pasture. Ten thousand people came out to hear me."

Listen, dear friends, they preached against sin. I have been reading about Sam Jones. God bless him! I don't know how he escaped with his life. I really don't. I don't know how he made it.

And Billy Sunday. Ma Sunday used to tell me when Billy Sunday went to town for a campaign, the ministerial association didn't meet him at the plane; the police department did. She said the poor fellow had to have protection or they would kill him on the way to his hotel room. That was Billy Sunday. Compare that to this popular kind of stuff we have today, if you please.

Take men like Jonathan Edwards. The first church he had, he was voted out because he preached against dancing.

Take John Wesley. He is still indicted in the state of

Georgia for slapping the Lord's Supper glass out of a lady's hand while she was taking it, because she was crooked.

When I was a kid, in Texas, there was old B. B. Crim. Now B. B. Crim had a lot of faults. He had too many hound dogs! But, my, how old B. B. Crim could preach! One time he had set a big tent up on the corner of Montana and Marsalis in Dallas. He dared the preachers not to co-operate. Old B. B. Crim set his tent up, got up and dared folks not to like it.

One night he preached on the second coming of Jesus Christ. I never will forget it. He scared me to death. I was a little kid about eleven years old, and lost. I went to hear him and he said, "Jesus is coming before Christmas." He hadn't read your book on Signs or No Signs, Dr. Rice! But he said, "Jesus is coming before Christmas. You had better get ready."

I thought everything the preacher said was true; so I said, "Mamma, I didn't know that, did you?"

She said, "No, I didn't, Son."

I said, "Is He really coming before Christmas?"

She said, "I guess He is; the preacher said He was."

That was September; I only had three months to get saved!

B. B. Crim said: "He is going to come and with a shout." Then I could hear the shout, and the trump. Then he said, "The dead in Christ will arise." Boy, I could just see the dead taking off and the tombstones rolling! Then he said, "We which are alive are going to be caught up like this"--he ducked down behind the choir rail, walked out the back of the tent and was gone.

I said, "Mamma, where did he go?"

She said, "Son, I don't know."

He ran all the way around that tent, and God knows, that was the longest sixty seconds I ever spent in my life. He scared me to death. Boy, by the time he got back to the side, I was almost converted! I got converted in a few days, I guarantee you that.

All of these old preachers, reckless men of God, abandonment of self and abandonment of popularity and abandonment of praise of the ministerial association. They didn't care--just the breath of God, and the anointing of God, and the power of the Holy Ghost, and to see sinners saved, and to preach against sin. Oh, how these men used to preach! They dug deeply these old wells of preaching against sin.

One Preacher Who Preached Pointedly to Sinners

There is a fellow down in Texas who doesn't know a thing about the second coming of Christ, but he hates sin. Oh, how he hates sin! One night he preached in an outdoor campaign sort of like this, in a tent with the flaps up. A great crowd came. The meanest man in the neighborhood was there. He brought his wife to church and sat out in the truck in the back. The preacher said, "Turn the P. A. system louder." They did. This man had been beating his wife, drinking liquor, and starving his kids. The preacher preached that night on:

> "Why Men Who Beat Their Wives and Drink Liquor and Starve Their Kids and Drive Their Wives to Church in a Truck and Sit Back in the Back, in a Truck Cab During the Service, Will Go to Hell if They Don't Get Born Again."

The next night the fellow got out and sat on the truck fender. When the preacher got up he said, "Tonight, folks, I am going to preach on the subject,

> "Why Men Who Beat Their Wives, Starve Their Kids, Drink Their Liquor, Come to Church One Night and Sit in the Cab, and the Next Night They Are on the Fender of the Truck--Why They Will Go to Hell if They Don't Get Born Again."

And the next night the fellow came again. This time he leaned against the tent post back in the back corner. The preacher got up and said, "My sermon topic tonight is,

> "Why Men Who Beat Their Wives and Starve Their Kids and Drink Their Liquor, and Sit One Night in the Cab and One Night on the Fender and One Night Against the Post Right Back Yonder--Why They Will Die and Go to Hell if They Don't Get Born Again."

The next night the fellow sat on the back row and he preached on the subject,

> "Why Men Who Drink Their Liquor and Beat Their Wives and Starve Their Kids and Sit in the Cab One Night and on the Fender the Next Night, Against the Tent Post the Next Night and on the Back Row the Next Night, Will Die and Go to Hell if They Don't Get Born Again."

The next night this meanest man in town was right here on the front row. And the preacher rose and preached on the subject,

> "Why Men Who Beat Their Wives and Starve Their Kids and Drink Their Liquor and Sit in the Cab One Night, on the Fender the Next Night and Against the Tent Post the Next Night and on the Back Row Last Night and Tonight Right Here--Why They Will Die and Go to Hell if They Don't Get Born Again."

Bless God, that man got born again!

I am not suggesting that you preach a revival campaign with those subjects, but I am saying that you had better not be too big a coward to do it, if God speaks to your heart about it.

These men brought tears. These little sissies who can't baptize anybody because they are not strong enough to baptize them! They get in the pulpits and preach little sermonettes to little Christianettes and smoke their cigarettes and have their sextets and octets, then go home, and there is no breath of God there. Why? You can't get a man saved until you get him lost--that is why. You can't get him lost until you can convince him he is a dirty, Hell-bound sinner.

So the Philistines have filled the well. They have filled it to our remorse. Brother, you can say what you want to say; you can holler it or you can whisper; you can bellow it or you can talk gently, you can do it with the finest of the theologians or with the most crude of us, but I will guarantee you one thing: if we don't learn to condemn and fight sin again, if we don't have some conviction of sin and preaching against sin in the 1960's and 1970's, by 1973 the communistic schedule will be fulfilled and America will be gone.

The trouble with our country is not the Democrats; it is sin. I enjoyed the little article you had in THE SWORD about the fellow in the business of not growing hogs. I laughed myself sick about that thing of not raising pigs. But that is not the trouble with our country. The trouble is sin.

Preaching Determines the Destiny of a Country

Did you know that the clergy and ministry of every country in history has determined the future and the destiny of that country? John Wesley and Charles Spurgeon did more to steer the destiny of England than all the politicians and queens and kings put together.

John Calvin did more for Geneva; Martin Luther did more for Germany; Dwight Moody and Billy Sunday did more for America; Charles G. Finney and Jonathan Edwards did more for our country than all the politicians put together, because the most powerful force in the world is the pulpit in our church. And if we don't return to preaching against sin and dig these wells deep again, God in Heaven help us! So I say, Let's do it again.

Tonight I looked at Dr. Rice. Dr. Rice has done more for me than I could ever deserve. Sometimes I wish he wouldn't be quite as kind. I feel so guilty. But he has been so good to me. And I wouldn't pad his pocket--he knows it. If I thought he was doing something wrong, I would skin him just like I would skin you, and I mean it. I would, and he knows I would. If I ever get afraid of Dr. Rice or anybody else, I am sunk. So are you. But I want to say this: To me Dr. Rice represents an era. To me he represents a trend. To me Dr. Rice is the nearest thing we have to a prophet in 1961 in our country. He is the nearest thing we have that is not afraid of anybody. He doesn't ask, "Who is there?" before he shoots. When he walks guard, he shoots, then says, "Who did I hit?" Most of us say, "Who is there?" If the answer is, "Somebody famous"--"Oh, pass on." "Who is there?" "A little bitty peon." Bang! Not Dr. Rice. He says, "Bang! Who died?"

I sat and watched him tonight. His hair is not black anymore; it is turning gray. He is not as strong as he used to be. I pray every day of my life, "Lord God, take care of John Rice." What are we going to do without him? What are we going to do when John Rice and Bob Jones pass off the scene? When these old men of God who have digged the wells and have given their lives and their future and their popularity and their prestige--what are we going to do when they pass on? We little sissy fellows who won't even buck the ministerial association in our town of a thousand people when these men fight the international battle for God--what are we going to do? We had better go well digging. We had better redig the wells of preaching against sin.

Some of you folks tonight, in your lives there was a day when you confessed your sin, there was a day when you went to God like Isaiah did and said, 'Lord, who am I for I am undone, for my eyes have seen the Lord.' There was a day when you went to church and when the preacher preached on sin, you saw your dirty, black, rotten sin standing between you and God and you came and confessed your sin and knelt at the mourner's bench and got right with God. Yet today I stand in the First Baptist Church of Hammond and bellow and holler and scream like a fog horn and I can't get two or three Christians even to admit that they have done anything wrong in the last several days. You can't get two or three Christians to see that they have done anything wrong in the last six months.

What is wrong? We are becoming sin-hardened. Preachers haven't digged the well of sin-fighting. When they do, some old long-nosed, crooked-spine deacon gets up and says, "I make a motion he resign." And the preacher says, "I guess my work is finished." Brother, I would begin a new work on him right quick. God must be sick of godly preachers letting a bunch of worldly deacons operate and run them around anyhow.

One of the curses of America is that the preacher thinks he is hired by the board of deacons. God give us free preachers. God give us sin-fighting, sin-hating, sin-condemning preachers who when they look at a world going to Hell, a world plunging into sin, a world of juvenile delinquency, a world of liberal churches, have their hearts broken to the place where they cannot help but preach against the sins around.

Some Reasons to Hate Sin

I recall when my father passed away. My father was a drunkard. I got the word he had passed away. My sister and I went to a little one-room apartment where he had lived. We got the little gatherings that Dad had left. He didn't leave us a dime, not a penny of insurance, not a thing, just an old souvenir of a gun, and one change of clothes and a funeral bill of seven hundred dollars. We went to that apartment and got his little clothes. You could put them all in my arms. That is a picture of what sin will do. One day he was a fine young man. He had owned a nice grocery store. Then sin came into his life and he died with nothing but a few pennies in his pocket, a hammer and a saw, a little gun, and one change of clothes.

When my sister and I went to his room early one Sunday morning to get the few things he left, a man who didn't know that Dad had passed away of a heart attack the day before [they called Dad "Pop"], came swaggering in and said, "Hello there. How are you?"

I said, "Fine."

He said, "Is Pop here?"

"No," I said, "Pop is not here. He won't be coming back."

"Well, do you see that whiskey bottle? See it?"

"Yes, I see it." (The whiskey bottle was over there in the corner.)

He said, "Me and Pop killed that whiskey bottle yesterday."

I picked up that whiskey bottle, looked at him and said, "Sir, that whiskey bottle killed Pop right after he killed the bottle." It was all I could do to keep from hitting that fellow in the head with it.

Tonight I hate liquor like I hate a rattlesnake. I hate any kind of liquor. I hate Martinis, I hate cocktails, I hate beer, I hate 3-2, I hate Seagrams Seven, I hate Four Roses --I hate it all. Why? Because I have seen what it will do to homes. I saw the wrinkles it put in my little mother's face. I saw the gray hairs it put in her head, and the stooped shoulders it caused. I saw her go to bed weeping at night because her boy and girl had no food to eat. The husband had drunk it all up. I hate it.

Let me tell you something else, dear friend. I hate sin. Sin caused the nails in Jesus' hands. Sin caused the spikes in His feet.

It was my sin and your sin that drove the crown of thorns down upon His precious brow.

It was my sin and your sin that caused the spittle and the slapping and the mockery.

It was my sin and your sin that caused the beating and the scourging when the cat-o'-nine tails went across His back nine times.

It was my sin and your sin that put the old cross on His back and caused Him to be so marred you could not even tell He was a man.

It was my sin and your sin that put Him on the cross and put the nails in His hands.

It was my sin and your sin that ripped the flesh as they lifted Him high above the earth and put the cross down in the socket, and as it hit He began to rip in His hands and feet. My sin and your sin caused that.

I tell you, don't you come wiggling your little old back up to me and say, "I love Jesus Christ" unless you have a bitter hatred for the sin that nailed Him to Calvary.

I say to us preachers, "Let's go to our pulpits next Sunday and let's preach against sin." I don't mean with a sarcastic delight that sin is sin; I mean with a heart that is broken because boys and girls, men and women, are plunging toward Hell and know not their need of salvation because we have not reminded them that they are sinners.

II. THE WELL OF BEER-SHEBA--A PROMISE OF GOD

The second well I call your attention to is the well of Beer-sheba. The word Beer-sheba means a promise of God or the Word of God.

Lately I have been reading a book of John Wesley's sermons. They are filled with Scripture.

When Jonathan Edwards preached "Sinners in the Hands of an Angry God," people cried out with conviction and grabbed the pillars of the building and begged for God not to let them drop into Hell.

Charles G. Finney went to a prayer meeting in Rochester, New York. They were having the prayer meeting in the basement of a church, so Finney got up and walked out, saying, "I am not going to stay in this prayer meeting. You are a bunch of hypocrites." The people got mad and began to walk out. The last one that walked out turned and said, "You are right. Let's come on back in and get right with God." They had a revival campaign. The power of God came.

Those old men preached the Bible. They didn't preach about "How Far It Is to Mars," about "How Shepard Got Up There and Back." Brother, they preached the Bible.

Preaching on Girl Scouts Instead of the Bible!

I heard a preacher on the radio today. He said, "I was on vacation recently, and I hungered to hear a blessed man of God walk in the pulpit and preach the Word of God. As I got out of the car and looked for a place to go to church, I saw a steeple. I saw people gathering, so I got my Bible and walked to the church to hear the blessed Word of God preached again. My heart was hungry." But he said, "The preacher got up and do you know what he preached on? It was Girl Scout Sunday, so he preached on 'How to be a good Girl Scout.' " This radio preacher said, "Ladies and gentlemen, I always try to apply the sermon to my own heart and do what it says. In seven days since I heard the sermon I can honestly say I have tried to do what the preacher said, but try as I may, work as I might, it is impossible for me to ever become a Girl Scout!"

O God, take us back to the Book again. God, help us to open the Bible and preach the Bible again.

Everybody is wanting something new. Folks come to me and say, "Brother Hyles, have you any new method?" What they mean is, "Have you any new gadgets? Got a little boomerang you can throw out so the kids will like it and flock to Sunday School?" That is what they want. But what they need is the Book.

I Learned to Preach the Book

I learned a long time ago to love the Book. The old-timers preached on Hell, judgment, salvation and Heaven. The Philistines have filled it up.

When I began preaching I didn't know any Bible. I knew one Scripture, John 3:16. I had two sermons; one was on cigarettes, the other on movies! I pastored a church and didn't know a single Scripture by heart but John 3:16. On Sunday morning I would preach on cigarettes; Sunday night, on the movies. The next Sunday I had a little variety. I would preach on the movies on Sunday morning, and cigarettes on Sunday night! I didn't have very many folks saved, but nobody in our church went to the movies or smoked cigarettes! We had a pretty clean church.

I began preaching. The chairman of the deacons and the Sunday School superintendent and the treasurer didn't want me in the church. So my first Sunday up there, there they sat out in front making faces at me on Sunday night. I was just a kid preacher. They thought I was too young. I thought I was, too, but I didn't tell them! They thought I didn't know enough Scripture. Why, I knew John 3:16 all the way through! And they thought I was inexperienced! I had been to college two weeks. What more experience could you want! I went to preaching and looked out and there they sat, right here in the middle and looking up at me. I said, "Dear Lord, what am I going to do?" There they sat; hissing out there in the crowd. I looked down at my Bible, then looked up. There they were. I would preach and look at my Bible; there they were again. I would look down and look up; there they were again.

Finally I just kept looking at my Bible and preaching and didn't even look up anymore. Brother, there it was in plain view! I said, "Praise the dear Lord in Heaven!" Do you know what I saw? A Scripture in Ezekiel that said, "Be not dismayed at their faces." Man, I looked up and said, "Glory to God! You three men out there in the middle--you have been making faces at me all during the service and I have been scared to death. But God gave me a Scripture right here in the Bible, 'Be not dismayed at their faces.'" I said, "Fasten your seat belts; the ride is going to be rocky from here on in."

The Bible Has the Answer to Every Problem

Brother, listen to me! I have found in these fifteen years of preaching the Gospel that the Word of God has the answer for every problem. The blessed truth of God's Word will meet every need you have in your pulpit, in your life, in your church, in your ministry.

Ah, the Bible! How many times have you gone home at night with a heavy heart! Oh, we cut up a great deal here. Dr. Rice says a lot of funny things. Bill Rice says more funny things than anybody I know. We cut up some here, but many nights our pillows are wet with tears. Any preacher worth his salt cries himself to sleep a lot of times. But how sweet it has been to open the Bible when your heart is broken and read in Revelation where Jesus holds His preachers and His messengers in His right hand. How sweet it is when we have to look in the face of a loved one, breathing no more, to read the Scripture, "Let not your heart be troubled: ye believe in God, believe also in me" (John 14:1). How many folks have found strength when they heard, "He that dwelleth in the secret place of the most High shall abide under the shadow of the Almighty" (Ps. 91:1).

Have you learned to love the Book, dear friends? Some of you ladies ought to go home, take all those True Romances and True Confessions, all those sexy novels, and burn them up, and read through the book of Genesis before you read another magazine or newspaper. Some of you men ought to get rid of the Esquire and some calendars, get rid of all those movie ads, all those sexy pin-up pictures, all those True Detective mysteries, turn your television off for a few days, get on your face before Christ and read the Bible again.

These old men of God preached the Bible and the breath of God came. Why! The Word of God was sweet. The Philistines have come along and said, "Oh yes! The Bible is a very good book, but Hell is not hot anymore. Heaven does not have golden streets anymore. The Bible is the Word of God, but not the inspired Word of God verbally; it is the thought."

Away with all that foolishness that God inspired the thoughts and men put it down in their own words. Away with all the foolishness that Hell is only separation from God, not fire.

In many fundamental circles today, the Philistines have filled up the well of Hell-fire. Many preachers who go under the name of fundamentalist and conservative Baptists say they believe in Hell, but they don't believe in Hell-fire and brimstone anymore. They believe that Hell is separation from God. Many of them say it may not be fire. But brother, the Bible says it is fire.

Some of you preachers are about like I was when I was fourteen. Mamma got real stupid when I was fourteen; then she had real failings mentally. When I got fifteen, Mamma was really about ready for the asylum. When I was sixteen, Mamma was as crazy as a bat. At seventeen, I was ashamed to let her out on the street. But at eighteen, I saw a little improvement. At nineteen, considerable improvement. At twenty, she was almost normal again. And tonight Mamma is smarter than she ever was. It is amazing how Mamma changed in those years. No, Mamma didn't change at all; I changed.

We have a bunch of little fourteen-year-old theologians, little teen-age theologians who think God is sort of crazy now, who think they know more than God knows. They won't be in Hell five minutes until they change their theological dissertations about Hell.

The Philistines have filled up the wells of the Word of God and the promise of God. Let's dig again.

The Lord Jesus, Hero of the Bible

The reason I love the Bible is because it is about Jesus. A fellow asked not long ago, "How many Messianic psalms are there?"

I said, "All of them."

He asked, "How many gospels in the Bible?"

I said, "Sixty-six."

He said, "Have you read the four gospels?"

"I have read sixty-six gospels. Every book in the Bible is about Jesus."

In Genesis, He is the Promised Seed that is going to come and bruise the head of the serpent.

In Exodus, He is the Passover Lamb.

In Leviticus, He is the Scapegoat.

In Numbers, He is the brazen serpent.

In Deuteronomy, He is the Great Lawgiver.

In Joshua, He is the Great Deliverer of Israel.

In Judges, He is the coming Judge who will judge the world.

In Ruth, He is kinsman Redeemer.

In Samuel, He is Prophet, Priest and King.

In Kings, He is King of kings and Lord of lords.

In Chronicles, the great historian.

In Ezra, He is the great rebuilder of the wall.

In Nehemiah, He is the great rebuilder of the temple.

In Esther, He is the Saviour and Deliverer of Israel.

In Job, He is the Friend that sticketh closer than a brother.

In the Psalms, He is the greatest song of the ages.

In Proverbs, He is the truth.

In Ecclesiastes, He is the preacher.

In the Song of Solomon, He is the great lover.

In Isaiah, He is Wonderful, Counsellor, Prince of Peace, the Mighty God, the Everlasting Father.

In Jeremiah, He is the Weeping Prophet.

In Lamentations, He is outside the city saying, "Is it nothing to you, all ye that pass by?"

In Ezekiel, He is the temple rebuilder.

In Daniel, He is the stone cut out without hands to come and break in pieces the stones of this world and kingdoms of this world and establish a kingdom that shall cover the earth as the waters cover the sea.

In Hosea, He is the great spurned lover.

In the minor prophets, He is the One coming in Bethlehem of Judaea.

In Matthew, He is King of kings and Lord of lords.

In Mark, He is the Suffering Servant.

In Luke, He is Son of man.

In John, He is the Son of God.

In Acts, He is the power of the church.

In the epistles, He is the root of the church.

In Jude, He is the One who is able to keep you from falling and present you faultless before the presence of His glory with exceeding joy.

In Revelation, He is the great cavalry leader who will saddle a white horse and lead all the host of Heaven back to establish a kingdom on this earth for a thousand wonderful, glorious years.

I say, from Genesis 1:1 to Revelation 22:21 is one big book and picture of our wonderful Lord and Saviour. Let's read about it, love it, live it, digest it, memorize it, meditate on it. Let us make this Bible our portion day after day. God help us to dig the wells of the Word of God.

The Well of Rehoboth--Fruitfulness

The third well Abraham digged was the well of Rehoboth. The word Rehoboth means fruitful, fruitfulness.

Those old settlers back in the early days of our country were soul winners. One of the sweetest stories is one Dr. Rice tells about Gipsy Smith. Dr. Rice went to hear Gipsy Smith in Dallas, Texas. Gipsy Smith preached on soul winning. They had an intermission in the service. Dr. Rice slipped outside of the building, thinking, "I ought to witness to someone after that great sermon by Gipsy Smith." Dr. Rice saw a taximan on the street. He walked up and asked, "Sir, are you a Christian?" The man said, "Yes, I became a Christian just a minute ago. A little fellow with gray hair and a mustache came out the side door which the speakers had gone in and told me about Jesus, and I just got converted."

Wouldn't it be wonderful if God would raise up some more Gipsy Smiths today? Wouldn't it be wonderful if God would raise up some soul-winning places like the famous old churches, which have just about had their wells filled today? Old Paul Rader's Tabernacle where once the breath of God was, and A. B. Simpson's Tabernacle--and others. I would love to have heard one of these great old men stand up and preach the Gospel and see sinners come down all these aisles, repenting of sin and confessing sin. But somehow or other the Philistines have about filled all the wells up that our fathers have digged.

Dear friends, if we have any wells in the next generation, do you know who is going to have to dig them? I am going to have to dig some; you are going to have to dig some.

One of the best things to me about these old men, the old prophets, is that they were all human just like I am. Old Wesley and Whitefield got in a fuss; so they encourage me a little bit. They got in a fuss with each other; couldn't get along with each other. One of them believed in predestination; the other didn't. They couldn't get along. It blessed me to find that they were human. And you know what could bring revival? If I would just get my pick and shovel and go well digging again. Get your Testament out tomorrow and let's go down to Murfreesboro and walk up and down the streets witnessing and battle the town for God, then go back home and preach soul winning on Sunday.

One fellow saw me in Kansas. He said, "Brother Hyles, I heard you and Dr. Rice and the fellows in the conference in Murfreesboro last year. We baptized only two people all the year long, but the next Sunday after I went home we had ten saved that Sunday morning." I am saying, go back home with the breath of God and the anointing of God and say, "Well, I am going to win people to Jesus." Dig the well of fruitfulness in your neighborhood, and by God's grace and mercy it will catch on. God can give us fruitfulness again in our country.

So Abraham digged the well of fruitfulness. Our old-timers are gone. The Philistines have filled it. Let's dig it again.

Abraham, the well of sin, preaching against sin, a God who sees and hears, a well of the promise of God, the well of fruitfulness.

God Showed Me That Soul Winning Is the Main Thing

When I began preaching I was like everybody else. I thought the world was waiting for me to open and blossom and that I would cure all the ills. I never will forget it. I preached and I preached, but nothing happened. For six months I had one convert and she was too little to get baptized. I used to say, "Dear Lord, remember me? I am Jack Hyles, the fellow that was going to pastor the First Baptist Church of Dallas. I am down here in Red River County, Morris Chapel Baptist Church in Bogota, Texas. Lord, don't forget me down here. I am still here, Lord." I used to get out under the shade of a tree and say, "Lord, where is the Lord God of Elijah?" When I preached nothing happened. And I wondered what was wrong. I used to pray in the middle of the night, "Where is the Lord God of Elijah?"

I went back to my little country church asking God to make me a soul winner. I went back to Grange Hall Baptist Church the next Sunday. That night I got to preach, and the floodtides of Heaven began to turn loose. I preached a simple message--I don't know what it was on. Maybe it was Elijah or something. When I got through preaching I gave the invitation and three people came to Jesus. Three. That was three times as many as I had had the first six months! I was so happy.

Down in East Texas we voted them in on the spot. Then we would sing, "Shall We Gather at the River?" and folks would come by and shake their hands, then go back to their seats. Then we had the closing prayer. And the crowd was gone.

Folks were leaving the service and I was so happy! I was still standing at the altar rejoicing in the Lord that three people got saved. I was in ecstasy. All of a sudden from behind me a great big 235-pound fellow hit me from the rear. He was draped all over me. "Brother Hyles, my 17-year-old daughter wants to get saved. Will you go talk to her?" I didn't walk down the aisle; I walked across the pews! I told her about Jesus and she got converted.

I went out on the front porch and said, "Hey, come on back in folks! Barbara got saved!" And the folks got out of their cars and came back in the church house, and we voted Barbara in. They came to shake her hand. We all waited, then had the benediction. Boy, that was wonderful! I said, "This is tremendous! Praise God!"

We dismissed the service, and I was at the altar rejoicing when all of a sudden the same fellow--wham! He hit me from the rear. "Brother Hyles, my other married daughter wants to get saved. Can you go and tell her?" I went back in the corner and told her about Jesus and got her saved, then went out on the front porch and said, "Hey, come on back in!" And they came back in, voted her in, came by to shake her hand. We dismissed the service again. Oh, I rejoiced in God!

Then about the time the folks got in their cars, the same fellow hit me and said, "Hey preacher! Her husband wants to get saved, too." I went back and got my arm around him, got him converted, then went out on the porch and said,

"Come on back in again." The folks came back in, we voted same in, they came by to shake his hand. Six saved!

Again I was standing at the altar after the dismissal prayer. The same fellow hit me again. He draped around me and said, "Preacher, I think I will get saved myself before I go home"! We knelt at the altar in the old church and I told somebody to go out and tell the people to come on back in; that another had gotten converted. It was 11:20 that night when we got through.

We went home, next door. The parsonage was a little old cheap place. We both couldn't get in the back bedroom at the same time--it would fall in. I am not kidding you. The front bedroom was fine, but if we had company, it had to be one at a time, because two people couldn't get in the back bedroom. Mrs. Hyles and I got our Bible, we opened it up and I said, "Honey, this is what I want every Sunday, don't you?" She said, "Yes." Two little old kids who didn't know John 3:16 very good--we got on our knees, opened the Bible, put our hands on the blessed Word of God and said, "Dear Lord, we are not going to have anything but this. We claim it."

We haven't had that every Sunday, but there has only been three Sundays in these fourteen years that we haven't seen somebody come to Christ in our ministry. Our little girl Becky is nine years old and she has never lived a Sunday without seeing somebody saved. Last Sunday morning we didn't have anybody saved in our church, which was so strange. One man came by letter. It was the Fourth of July week end. Normally we would have had fifteen or twenty and everything was peculiar. I went home and my wife said, "Honey, what are you going to do?" I said, "I am going to visit."

I got in my car and visited up and down the streets all afternoon. I said, "Dear Lord, Becky don't know what it is ...Becky has never gone to church a Sunday without seeing somebody converted. Dear Lord, don't let Becky have an old cold, dead daddy for a preacher." And Sunday night the aisle was filled and people got saved.

By My Father's Grave

A few weeks ago I went back to Texas. I went fifty miles south of my home in Dallas to a little town called Italy, Texas, where a tornado hit recently and blew the town's main street away. I went to a little cemetery on the highway (the highway curves around the cemetery), and in the gate, away down to a little creek that ends at the cemetery and on the bank of that creek is a little tombstone that I bought. On it is the name of Willis Athey Hyles, born 1887; died May 13, 1950. I got on my knees at the old tombstone and said, "Dear Lord, in 1950 I knelt here and something happened to me. Do it again! Do it again!"

Christians, Clean Out Your Wells

A lot of you folks tonight need to have it done again. Your wells are full, stopped up. You haven't read the Bible. You used to love it. Its pages were fresh. The Word of God used to be your portion. You don't read it much anymore. The Philistines have come and stopped up your well. Dig it deep tonight! Dig it deep tonight! A lot of you used to witness. You used to carry tracts in your pocket and walk down the street and pass out tracts. You used to tell folks about Jesus and you weren't ashamed of it. But the Philistines have come and stopped the wells. Get the old spiritual pick and shovel and dig it deep tonight. Dig it deep.

A lot of you used to have confession of sin. You were ashamed of your sin. You saw the Lord and you said, "Woe is me, for I am undone." The Philistines have stopped it up. Dig it deep! Dig it deep! If we don't have some well-digging done, the next decade the wells will be stopped up for good in our country. If we young preachers--and when I say young I don't mean that we are too young--if those of us in our thirties and twenties and forties don't get out with shovels and picks that these old men of God used to have,

God's wells will be filled up in America. We should walk with John Rice and Bob Jones and others and say, "O. K. fellows, the old shovel is getting heavy, the old pick is getting heavy. Let us have it. Let us help you." Let us dig awhile and let's dig deeply the wells that these men of God have dug through the years. God help us to have some well digging across the country.

You say, "How can the Christian climate improve?" It improves as in this conference we dig some wells; as up in Ohio the folks dig some wells; as in the next conference we dig some wells; as up north some folks dig some wells; as in the next conference and down in Danville, Illinois, the next Sword conference some folks dig some wells; as up in Winston-Salem tonight in the conference they are having some folks dig some wells. Then next Sunday morning fifty preachers go back to fifty churches or more who are here tonight and get up before the people and say, "Folks, a new man is in the pulpit again," and as we preach against sin and preach about soul winning and get back in the Word of God and our people start digging wells again--that is the way it can happen.

Let me have your attention: the other day I picked up a poem and I read it and I memorized it. You know it.

An old man, traveling a lone highway,
Came at the evening cold and gray,
To a chasm deep and wide,
Through which was flowing a sullen tide.

The old man crossed in the twilight dim,
For the sullen stream held no fears for him.
But he turned when he reached the other side,
And builded a bridge to span the tide.

"Old man," cried a fellow pilgrim near,
"You are wasting your strength with building here;
Your journey will end with the ending day,
And you never again will pass this way.

"You have crossed the chasm deep and wide.
Why build you a bridge at eventide?"
And the builder raised his old gray head:
"Good friend, on the path I have come," he said,
"There followeth after me today
A youth whose feet will pass this way.

"This stream, which has been as naught to me,
To that fair-haired boy may a pitfall be;
He, too, must cross in the twilight dim--
Good friend, I am building this bridge for him."

Let's build some bridges, dig some wells, and go deep in the Word of God. Have you confessed your sin? Have you been reading the Bible? Have you been witnessing? Don't you feel you ought to do some well digging? I do.

Our Father, help us in the name of Christ to dig some wells. In Jesus' name, Amen.

2

Why Jesus Wept

"When the Lord turned again the captivity of Zion, we were like them that dream. Then was our mouth filled with laughter, and our tongue with singing: then said they among the heathen, The Lord hath done great things for them. The Lord hath done great things for us; whereof we are glad. Turn again our captivity, O Lord, as the streams in the south. They that sow in tears shall reap in joy. He that goeth forth and weepeth, bearing precious seed, shall doubtless come again with rejoicing, bringing his sheaves with him."--Ps. 126:1-6.

"Then when Mary was come where Jesus was, and saw him, she fell down at his feet, saying unto him, Lord, if thou hadst been here, my brother had not died. When Jesus therefore saw her weeping, and the Jews also weeping which came with her, he groaned in the spirit, and was troubled, And said, Where have ye laid him? They said unto him, Lord, come and see. Jesus wept."--John 11:32-35.

To me the most marvelous thing about these Scriptures is that our Saviour was touched with our infirmities. Jesus wept, as far as I can see in the Bible, about only three things. And I want to discuss these things with you tonight as we think on the subject, "Jesus Wept."

When I first went to college, I enrolled in the East Texas Baptist College in Marshall, Texas. I had already had a year in a state college. I was called to a little half-time country church way up in Red River County, the Morris Chapel Baptist Church, where I was for awhile. The church was a hundred miles from the college. We lived in Marshall and Red River County was about a hundred miles from where we lived. I had Wednesday nights off. I love to preach. Somebody said yesterday, "Are you tired? You drove all night, night before last." (I preached yesterday morning and taught for two and a half hours yesterday afternoon and preached again last night.) No, I was dead-tired this afternoon after teaching. Teaching wears me out. But preaching is like pushing a car off. After you get it started, it regenerates itself. Preaching generates itself and keeps building up and reproducing energy. Teaching doesn't. I like to preach. I preach every chance I get. I can preach myself out of a backslidden condition better than any other way. If I get to preaching and get happy and rejoice, my old cold heart gets warm again.

Since my church was a hundred miles away, I wanted to find a place to preach on Wednesday night. I went out into the country. I came to a little church named St. Mary's Baptist Church. It was a little old leaning thing, a southern type church with a graveyard in the back. I hollered, "Hello! Hello!" (Now you folks who don't know what that means--that is ringing the doorbell where I was reared.)

A fellow answered, "Hello, yes sir; hello." (I didn't know it was a colored church.)

A man came around the corner of that little church and I said, "How do you do? My name is Jack Hyles, a preacher; I go to East Texas Baptist College, and I want to know if you folks have full-time preaching."

"Yes sir," he said. "We shore do have some full-time preaching."

Now where I came from some churches didn't have preaching every Sunday, but every other Sunday or once a quarter. So I asked, "Do you have preaching every Sunday?"

"Yes sir; we shore do. We have preaching every Sunday in the St. Mary's Baptist Church."

"Well," I asked, "do you have preaching on Wednesday night?"

"No sir, we don't have no preaching on Wednesday night."

I said, "How would you like to have it?"

"Well," he said, "I think we would like to have it."

I said, "I will tell you what I will do. It won't cost you a thing. I will come out every Wednesday night and preach to you folks, if you will hear me. You get the folks together and I will preach and it won't cost you a thing. I will meet you here about seven-thirty and talk to you every Wednesday night."

And he said, "Yes sir, that would be awful nice."

So I cut my preaching teeth out at St. Mary's Baptist Church, ten miles south of Marshall, Texas. Some of the greatest times I have ever had in my life were out in that church. I loved it.

I went out on Wednesday night. The front door of the church faced the west. I came up the road from the rear, turned around and parked in the church parking lot. The people would already be there. They never were late. They used coal oil lamps and lanterns but wouldn't light the lamps until the preacher got there.

I walked in the back door. I never knew how many folks were there until they turned around. I counted eyes and divided by two, you know! When I came in they would say, "Rev. Jack is here." The lamps would be lit and I would preach.

You think I am loud-mouthed! You think I get aroused a little bit now. Brother, the best preaching I ever did in my life was out in the St. Mary's Baptist Church!

I would preach. Brother, you talk about preaching! Every Wednesday night Deacon Bussy sat on the back row. We had maybe thirty present. I preached. I would hang from the rafters! I screamed, hollered, bellowed! After a while Deacon Bussy would get in the Spirit! His eyes got big, then he started rolling them! He forgot where he was. He would stand up, then the entire back row would stand. Then you could see about twenty eyes get as big as silver dollars and begin to roll. Old Deacon Bussy would step out in the aisle, taken by some strange force. I don't know what it was but I wish our First Baptist Church in Hammond would get it! He would begin to walk down the aisle. The man behind him would follow him out in the aisle, too. Finally the entire back row would be lined up facing toward the back. Then that next row in front of them would do the same thing, then the next row, and the next row. Finally everybody in that colored crowd were up on their feet with their eyes rolling. (A fellow said once, "I heard some shouting, but it was counterfeit." Well, I would just love to hear even some counterfeit shouting. I am so hungry for something besides this deadness.)

These colored folk would get out in the aisle. I have never danced a step in my life. I have never seen what they call a Conga line. Now that was what I would say a Conga line is like. The fellow behind Deacon Bussy put his hands on Deacon Bussy's waist. All of the men sat together and all the ladies sat together in that church--the men on one side and the ladies on the other. Those were the good old days! Finally they would all line up and each one would put his hands on the waist of the fellow in front of him, go around the building singing, "What could I do without the Lord!" Around and around that building they went singing and praising God and crying. Many a Wednesday night Jack Hyles, a young preacher--I didn't know any better; I still don't--would be on the tail end of that Conga line! Man, my eyes would roll and I sang, "What could I do without the Lord!"

There I Learned to Weep Before the Lord

You know, I learned something from that little place; something got in my bones there. That is why I am like I am now. Something got in my bones in that little old country church, with those colored folks rejoicing in the Lord. I mean they got happy. It was real. Many a night old Deacon Bussy and I would hug each other and rejoice in the Lord and praise God together. They knew how to weep. Those old darkies could cry. They would pray, and weep, and confess their sins. Brother, I could preach on any sin and everyone of them confessed it. I don't know how many of them committed it, but they would all confess it! Then they cried and wept; I would cry; we would confess and get right. And many a night, way in the night we would still be over there in the little colored church praising God together.

I would go back to school and hear those theologians speak and I would wish I were at St. Mary's.

Now I learned something. In the fifteen years I have been preaching, I have seen a transition from tears and weeping to dry-eyed Christianity, even in fundamental churches. I can recall when we had revival campaigns, everybody cried for sinners. Dear old saints of God, dear ladies, would come to the altar in every revival campaign and pray until morning, and cry for their husbands, their wayward sons, their wayward brothers and sisters. They wept because folks were lost. Yet today this fundamental deadness has set in, and there is nothing as dead as fundamental deadness. There is nothing as dry-eyed as to go to a liberal church that hasn't got anything, except to go to a fundamental church that hasn't got anything. And this fundamental, dry-eyed deadness has set in until today you can hardly find a place where people care enough about sinners to weep about them.

The other day I was in a home. Somehow I couldn't win the fellow to Christ. Before I knew it I was overcome and began to cry. Walking over to him with great big old tears rolling down my cheeks, I said, "You have just got to get saved!" He said, "All right, I will." He got saved. I am just saying, "They that sow in tears shall reap in joy." Brother, you have to water your crop if you are going to raise any fruit next year. You have to have some tears. The reason a lot of you folks who go out and knock on doors don't have anything happen, the reason a lot of you go downtown and witness and nothing happens, is because you don't care. You learn the mechanics, but there is no broken heart, no burden for sinners. Nobody seems to care any more.

In the little country church I used to pastor, we cared. Bill Harvey tells about the colored lady who was eating a watermelon when somebody came up and said, "Liza, your old man just died."

She said, "O. K." and kept on eating her watermelon.

So she again said, "Liza, your husband, he am dead."

She just kept eating her watermelon.

"Liza, I say, your husband, he is dead."

Liza looked up, "I know Matilda; when I get through eating this watermelon, you ain't never heard such carrying on as I am going to do!"

Down in East Texas you never heard such carrying on as we did.

Nowadays folks don't even cry at funerals. Folks don't care anymore. Some places it is counted a sin to cry. It is a sign of instability, a sign that you don't believe the Bible. Some think it is a sign of failure to cry. But the Bible still says, "They that sow in tears shall reap in joy. He that goeth forth and weepeth, bearing precious seed, shall doubtless come again with rejoicing, bringing his sheaves with him" (Ps. 126:5, 6). And "Jesus," the Bible says, "wept."

I have read some biographies of great men. I wonder sometimes where are the David Brainerds who will cry day after day. I wonder where are the John Welches who will get out of bed at night and scold their wives for rebuking their weeping. I wonder sometimes where are the Paysons whose knees leave grooves in the hardwood floors; or the John Fletchers who stain their walls with their breath as they pray every night; or the John Wesleys who arise at four o'clock in the morning and pray until six every morning; or the George Foxes who stay in a trance for days because they are so burdened for sinners; or the Jeremiahs who can be called the weeping prophets; or the Davids who say, "I water my couch every night with tears"; or the Jobs who say, "Mine eyes poureth out tears"; or Isaiahs who say, "I will water thee with my tears"; or psalmists who say, "They that sow in tears," or Apostle Pauls who say, "I ceased not to warn every one night and day with tears." I wonder sometimes where are the broken and contrite spirits we used to have in revival campaigns.

These evangelists can tell you. Dr. Bill Rice, Dr. John R. Rice, and Walt Handford can tell you. They can testify that every year it seems our eyes are getting dryer, and nobody seems to care.

Let me ask you a question: How long has it been since you cried? You can watch some television show, some picture show; your parakeet can die; your dog can get run over by a car, your old cat can have kittens born dead, and you will weep glycerin tears of sorrow. Yet sinners are going to Hell by the thousands and nobody seems to care. We will not have real revival in our churches until we care again about the condition of sinners.

"They that sow in tears shall reap in joy." Now what does Jesus mean by that? Only three things Jesus ever wept about. The Bible never says that Jesus wept because of harvest; it never says Jesus wept because of hungry people. The Bible never says that Jesus wept because of widows. It never mentions Jesus weeping because of the physical conditions of people. But the Bible does say that Jesus wept.

Jesus Wept Because of Death

Now what did Jesus weep over? He came to the grave of Lazarus who had been dead for four days. Even knowing that He was about to raise Lazarus from the grave, even realizing that Lazarus was going to live again in just a moment, the Bible says Jesus looked at the grave of Lazarus and "Jesus wept." Now Jesus wept because of death. Seeing people plunging toward Hell and dying in sin, Jesus wept. Don't you think, dear friend, that we ought to weep?

Lost Sinners Die All Around Us

I open the newspaper. I read the front page; the sport page; the want ads. I just love to read the want ads. Then I read the obituary every day, and wonder how many of those people were on my prospect file, how many of them could I have witnessed to and didn't.

A man in our town was killed, a policeman, at two o'clock in the morning, killed in cold blood, for no reason at all. Nothing was wrong. He was walking down his beat going to a laundrymat and just checking the front door to see if anybody was in there and somebody shot him in cold blood, and for no reason at all. I heard it on the broadcast about six o'clock in the morning. He was killed just about a block and a half from our church. I went to the church office and about ten o'clock Mrs. Kirk came rushing in panting to say, "Brother Hyles, the policeman who was killed was in our service last Sunday morning."

I went out and talked to Brother McKeighan, one of our deacons. He said, "Brother Hyles, I brought him to church last Sunday morning! He was my guest. He heard you preach the Gospel in the Sunday School hour and he heard you give the invitation, but he wasn't saved. He said 'no' to Jesus Christ. Someone asked him, 'Are you going to come back next Sunday?' And he said, 'I sure am.' 'Are you sure?' 'Yes, if I am not dead I will be there.'"

Tuesday morning he was gone. I preached to him. I am saying, someone ought to weep about things like this.

Somebody ought to care about people who come to hear us preach.

My folks ask me, "Brother Hyles, why is it every Sunday you try to get folks saved? Why is it every Sunday there is an invitation? Why is it other churches get home by twelve o'clock and we get home about 1:00 or 1:15 every Sunday? Why is it the other churches sing two stanzas of one song and we sing and sing and sing? Why can't we have a church like other churches, and a preacher like other preachers, and an invitation like other churches have?" I will tell you why. I don't know about your town, but folks in Hammond are dying and somebody is not going to get the Gospel again.

I recall other people tonight. A Mr. and Mrs. Berry heard me preach in Marshall, Texas. Mrs. Berry raised her hand for prayer and she said she was lost. He raised his hand. He did not see her; she did not see him. They were sitting side by side. She raised her right hand and he raised his left for prayer. They trembled but they didn't get saved. The next Friday morning Mrs. Berry shot Mr. Berry in cold blood while he was on his knees begging for mercy. And within two weeks she was killed in a car wreck. That was the last sermon they ever heard. And as far as I know they are in Hell tonight.

I am saying, my precious friends, somebody ought to cry because we are preaching to dying people.

We talk about formalism a great deal. I don't like formalism. Somebody said to me not long ago, "Did you ever see a new church that was formal? Did you ever see a new church under a brush arbor, and the preacher with a soap box for a pulpit, sing "The Lord Is in His Holy Temple"? Did you ever see a kid preacher with his first sermon go out in the country for an old-fashioned camp meeting and really get the power of God in his life and only knew one sermon and that was, "You have got to get born again or you are going to burn in Hell"--have you ever seen him stand up with a robe on and say, "Good morning, beloved, we are happy to have you"? No, deadness and formality come with age.

Somebody says, "Sure, you are like a little baby. A little baby cries, makes lots of noise, and says 'goo goo' and 'ga ga.' But when a baby gets mature, he gets quieter." No, it isn't because they mature; it is because the baby is dying. You see, as you get older you begin to die. I can't skip rope now because I have been dying for several years, and I am worn out. It is not because I am more mature. If I had the energy my little seven-year-old boy has, I would be just like he is. But the reason is, we are dying. Death sets in at birth. The reason churches get cold when they get old is because they begin to die. You have to fight against death with spiritual hypos and spiritual penicillin shots, or you are gone.

My precious friends, when the church of Jesus Christ gets her spiritual youth again, gets her spiritual vigor again, gets burdened again over sinners and the people come back to pray, to care, to weep about sinners, to get burdened because folks are dying near us, God will send revival.

So Jesus wept because of death.

Bobby Flowers was killed in a car wreck within two hours after he heard me preach. He said "no" to the Gospel.

There was Mr. Bloware. He sat near the back one night. I preached on "To Hell and Back." He heard me. He said, "No, I will not be saved." He walked out on Sunday night. On Tuesday at noon he was dead, thirty-nine years old.

There was Mr. White, forty-two years old. He heard me preach one time and he is now in Hell as far as I know.

Ah, a great line of people could march past me, step by step by step who have heard me preach, who have plunged into Hell. As you stand and look at your congregation on Sunday morning and remember that people sat in those very pews who are in eternity, not saved--if that doesn't drive you to burden and tears, something is wrong with your ministry. Jesus wept because of death.

The only sermons my father heard in the last five years of his life were two sermons by his own son. I have cried more tears over my dad than any other single thing in my life. I dream about him. I dream about that sermon I preached that Sunday morning, "What Must I Do to Be Saved?" I still relive the experience. Sometimes I wonder if I had just done a little better. My old one-legged chairman of the deacons put his arms around my old dad and said, "Mr. Hyles, won't you get saved today?" And Dad trembled in fear about his soul but he shook his head and said, "No." Of all the tears that I have cried since Daddy died--suppose I had cried all of those tears before he died!

Some of you folks have loved ones, and one of these days you are going to be like I am. You will cry yourself to sleep and be heartbroken because they are in Hell. You are going to wish you had cried before instead of later.

Dad heard me preach January 1, 1950. He never heard another sermon. He was gone before he ever heard another one.

Some We Have Won Are Already Gone to Heaven

I think also about the death of those I have led to Christ. I usually shout along here somewhere! There are people up in Heaven tonight whom I have sent up there. I mean they are in Heaven right now.

I get sick sometimes of this old world we live in. We get wrapped up in so many little old piddling things.

Here is a professional golfer. He can take a little white ball about an inch and a half in diameter, take a stick with a piece of steel on the end of it, and he can swing that stick and hit that ball and knock it away over a cow pasture into a little hole that has a flag over it some three hundred yards away, and he can do it in five licks. Everybody says, "Whooo! Isn't that wonderful!" We get so excited.

A ball player can swing a piece of wood, and hit a piece of horse skin and knock that horse skin over a fence and everybody says, "Whew!"

Here's a fellow who can take a piece of pig hide and blow it up with air and kick that thing fifty-two yards through a piece of pipe down the end of the field and everybody says, "Whew! Isn't that wonderful!"

No, that is piddling nonsense. When you can get on the ball for God and lead sinners to Jesus Christ, when folks can go to Heaven and live forever and walk down golden streets and have fellowship with Abraham, Isaac, Jesus and Jacob and Paul and Barnabas and Andrew and Peter and enjoy the fellowship of the angels and God for ever and ever, why in the name of common sense can't we Christians get some proper evaluation of what is eternal and right and good?

Oh, those people up in Heaven tonight! I went to the hospital one day to see Mr. Carter. His wife was beside him. "Mr. Carter, are you saved?"

"Nope, and I ain't gonna be." (Did you ever hear that before?)

"Mrs. Carter, are you saved?"

"Yes, I am saved," she said.

"Mr. Carter, could I tell you how to be saved?"

"Nope."

"Well, he had cancer and couldn't do anything about it; so I told him anyhow. And I said, "Now I am going to pray." When I prayed he started praying and saying, "It is wonderful!" I didn't know what he meant. He said, "It is wonderful!"

After a while I said, "Would you pray?"

He said, "Dear Lord..." and he punched me and said, "Brother Hyles, it is wonderful!" And he prayed, "Lord, have mercy on me a sinner. I trust You as my Saviour now." He said, "Brother Hyles, it sure is wonderful!"

Well, I agree, it is wonderful.

And he kept saying, "It is wonderful!"

Then I looked over at Mrs. Carter after he got saved and said, "You are already saved, aren't you?"

He answered for her. "No, she isn't saved. She hasn't got what I've got."

And she said, "I don't guess I have." So she started praying and while she was praying he was punching her in the ribs and saying, "Honey, I told you it was wonderful! I told you it was wonderful!"

Within three or four months Mr. Carter passed away. I had given him a little Testament as a souvenir. I hadn't seen him in a number of weeks. I went to conduct his funeral in another city where he had been transferred. I went to the funeral home. Instead of having his hands crossed like they do, underneath his right hand, right over his heart was the little brown Testament. His right hand was over the Testament and his left hand was over his right. I said, "Mrs. Carter, that's..."

"Yes," she said, "that is the way he requested it."

He is in Heaven tonight. He will be there a hundred years from tonight; a thousand years he will still be there. Man, that is big league! Ted Williams never did anything like that. That is something! That is real! You can break all the Sunday School records, but that won't take the place of this kind of thing. Oh, you can be the Associational Moderator; you can have all on the annual reports; you can give your reports--the number of churches warded. You can have warded more churches than any other missionary that ever warded a church, but you are not going to do something big until you get in this soul-winning business.

I picked up The Evangelist, Dr. Roberson's paper, and there was a picture of Marjorie Wiley Stuart, a faculty member of Tennessee Temple Schools. A few months after she married, she was going with a foreign girl to get her driver's license in a small foreign car and had a wreck, and Marjorie was killed. I got a letter from Mrs. Wiley, her mother:

"Dear Brother Hyles:

"Marjorie has gone to Heaven. She is there because you told her about Jesus."

Her mother went on to relive the experience.

I went out Centerville Road in the little old East Texas sand hills. I turned left off of the Centerville Road and went down the valley and up on top of the hill and around a little curve or two and there was a little house sitting way back on a sand hill in East Texas, away back off the lot. I knocked.

"Mrs. Wiley, I am Brother Hyles, pastor of a little country church down here on the highway."

Mrs. Wiley said, "I am happy to know you."

"I came, Mrs. Wiley, to talk to you about Jesus Christ."

Mrs. Wiley was saved as I talked to her. Later I led her husband to Jesus; I led her married daughter, Mrs. Martin, to Jesus. I led her football-player son, Tom Wiley, to Jesus. And as I started to leave the house, so happy I had won the family to Christ, a little girl over in the corner about nine years old said, as I recall, "Mr. Brother Hyles, you are not going to forget about me, are you?" In the corner was a sweet little blond-headed girl. I hugged her and said, "Sweetheart, I am not going to forget you." I knelt beside that precious little girl and told her the story of Jesus. That was Marjorie Wiley Stuart, later a faculty member at Tennessee Temple Schools, who is now in Heaven. I keep her picture on a little desk in my office. She is in Heaven, dear friends.

I wonder why you folks don't get in the biggest business in the world? Some of you folks this afternoon had time to go horseback riding, but you didn't have time to go soul-back riding. Oh, you can ride some old horse until you are sore and bowlegged, while sinners die and go to Hell. We don't care anymore.

Jesus Wept Because of Sin

And so Jesus wept about death. Jesus wept about sin. The Bible says outside the city of Jerusalem He looked out over the city and said, "O Jerusalem, Jerusalem...how often would I have gathered thy children together, even as a hen gathereth her chickens under her wings, and ye would not!" 'I wanted to pull you close to Me and love you; I wanted you to be Mine and live right, but you went your own way and you have gone into sin and have turned Me down.' Jesus wept tears of sorrow. He wept because of sin.

We Need Preachers Who Weep and Warn About Sin

Let me tell you something! If we don't raise a generation of preachers to whom sin is exceedingly sinful, we are in pretty sad shape. Ah, the exceeding sinfulness of sin!

A little girl came to my office a few months ago and said, "Brother Hyles, I am fourteen years old, and I have to quit junior high school and go away to a home for unwed mothers. I am going to have a baby."

After she left I got to thinking: she heard me preach every Sunday! She sang in the choir! Oh, I wish I had made sin blacker. I wish I had borne down a little more on getting with the wrong crowd. I wish I had gotten madder, harder, and meaner about running with the wrong boys and staying up until one o'clock in the morning.

She waved good-by to me as she walked off, to be gone for six or seven months to give birth to a little baby, to enter the jaws of death for a little baby's life she would never see.

A couple came not long ago to see me. The boy was fifteen, the girl fourteen. They said, "Brother Hyles, we have to get married."

I said, "Kids, why?"

"Brother Hyles, we have to get married."

I said, "What in the name of common sense possessed you to do something like this?"

Fifteen and fourteen years old, little kids who ought to be at home playing baseball and dolls, in sin! And we preachers get in our pulpits and act like all is right with the world. And if some little fellow gets fanatical and excited and burdened about sin and becomes a sin-fighter, the whole town is shocked and the old sisters lift their glasses, Mrs. Peabody loses her false teeth, and the bankers think somebody has gone crazy. Why? Listen, somebody had better get concerned about sin or our country and churches combined are going to the Devil fast. Jesus wept about sin.

One of the best missionaries I ever saw--we supported him, loved him--went to Mexico. He had three or four little precious children and a sweet wife. Some little old harlot down in Mexico winked at him and the Devil got him. He ran off from his wife and left his children, took an airplane which we helped buy with the sacrificial dollars of God's people, and with that little old Mexican gal went across the country and left the most precious possessions that God had given him.

I am saying that in a world where the preachers are running off with women in their church, where the average church deacons go dancing on Saturday night and sip cocktails, then take the collection on Sunday morning; where the Sunday School teachers can dance on Saturday night and teach on Sunday morning--and nobody seems to care! Jesus wept because of sin. He wept for sinners.

She Cared About Her Sinful Husband

When I was in East Texas a lady, Mrs. Ford, used to come to church. She used to kneel and pray at the altar: "Dear Jesus, save Jim." That was her drunkard husband. "Dear Jesus, save Jim." She would beg, "Save Jim." Many a night she would pray until one o'clock in the morning. We used to have all-night prayer meetings back in those days. And Mrs. Ford would crawl across the altar on her knees and--"Lord," she would say, "save Jim. O God, You had better save Jim! Lord, You have got to save old Jim!" We prayed and the church was brokenhearted.

On Christmas Eve we prayed for Jim. Christmas Eve was on Saturday and Christmas on Sunday that year. The next morning I was surprised when in walked Jim. That night he walked back in again. While I was preaching old Jim jumped up and said, "I am going to get saved now." He took off down the aisle, got on his knees, began to confess and got converted. Mrs. Ford jumped up out of the seat back there and started jumping up and down and saying, "Oh, thank You Jesus! Thank You, Jesus!" We just stopped the service. She came down the aisle hugging and kissing everybody. She was one of these fat, shouting kind! I weighed 141 pounds soaking wet. She picked me up and hugged me and lifted me up in the air and said, "Oh, thank You, Jesus! Thank You!" She cared about her husband.

Some of you ladies--all your husband ever hears is griping about the long sermon the preacher preaches on Sunday morning. He will die and go to Hell because of your gossiping tongue. Oh, she rejoiced and she wept.

"They that sow in tears shall reap in joy."

He Was Not Careful Enough!

I was in the paratroopers in World War II, in the riggers company. The riggers are those who pack the parachutes for the 82nd Airborne Division. We were called the Parachute Maintenance Company. We had a large hanger, and long tables in the hanger. Each man had a table on which to pack parachutes. We packed parachutes for all the men. On this side of me was a young man named Alley. Alley was killed while jumping. He jumped and hit a body of water and drowned. Another man on the other side of me was named Collingsworth, an eighteen-year-old kid from New Jersey, a fine, clear-cut kid. I was also eighteen. Collingsworth packed on the table adjacent to mine.

One time Captain Fuller called the company together and

said, "Men, in ten days the Mexican consul is coming to the States to review the paratroopers of the 82nd Airborne Division. We must pack all of the parachutes for the 82nd Airborne Division." General James Gavin, our commanding general, who is now the ambassador to France, said that we must pack enough chutes for the entire division. "You will have to work day and night to get it done."

Collingsworth, Alley and I began to pack the chutes for the division. We worked literally day and night, with only two or three hours' sleep a night.

The time came to jump. It is a wonderful thing. You ought to jump one time for the thrill of jumping. I wouldn't do it again for ten thousand dollars, but I am glad I did it. It was a thrill to me when I was a kid. Back in those days I loved to jump. We would get in the airplane, nine men on one side and nine men on the other in those C46's and C47's. The sergeant got over the landing field and the green light came up over where the pilot was and the sergeant said, "Stand up and hook up." So we stood up and each of us got in line and faced the back of the plane. Then the sergeant said, "Hook up." We took the static line, a line on the end of our parachute pack, and hooked it up to a cable over us. That cable would pull the parachute out and we didn't have to pull the ripcord on the main chute. And so we hooked up.

Then he said, "Check your equipment." We checked the equipment of the fellow in front of us. You couldn't check your own. The fellow behind checked the equipment of the fellow in front. I would turn around and say, "Boy, do a good job!" We checked the equipment.

Then the sergeant said, "Stand in the door." I was the first man to jump. So I stood in the door. Here is what you do. Put your hands like this on the outside of the plane. You always look toward the horizon, never down. If you ever look down, you will never jump! You look toward the horizon, bend your knees slightly, then the man says,

"Ready...jump." You answer, "Ready...jump." You take your left leg, put it even with your right, make a forty-five degree turn toward the rear of the plane, hug tightly your reserved parachute, put your chin down next to your body and roll up like this; then you count one thousand, two thousand, three thousand, then if everything is O. K. the parachute will open before you count four thousand; if not, you have a reserve chute you can pull.

So thc time came to jump. The Mexican consul was there. We jumped first because it was our job to gather all the chutes that had been used before. Collingsworth and I both jumped together, then we stood on the landing field and watched the fellows jump--a beautiful sight. As they jumped they would shout, "One thousand, two thousand, three thousand"--and the chutes would open. "One thousand, two thousand"--and another chute would open. You could see them twisting and turning; pretty soon the chute would open. It was a beautiful sight.

On the inside of the parachute was what was called a log book. Every time we packed a chute, we had to sign our name in the log book and put the date of the packing.

And we watched the fellows jump, then picked up the parachutes. We saw hundreds of fellows jump that day.

Then Collingsworth and I saw a man come out and count one thousand, two thousand, three thousand, four thousand, five thousand....He had what they called a streamer. And when you have a streamer, the parachute comes out of the pack, but the suspension lines wrap around the silk and it is just a straight long line, much like an exclamation mark, and the chute never opens. This fellow had a streamer and we saw him try to get his reserve chute--he only had eight seconds to do it. He actually had clawed through canvass and silk into his flesh, actually clawed into his stomach with his fingernails. He hit the ground with a thud.

Collingsworth and I ran quickly over to his body. By the time we got there the commanding officer was beside him.

He had gotten in his jeep and beaten us there. When we got there, with his feet the General was stirring the boy's body just like a bowl of soup. His bones were in thousands of pieces. His flesh was ripped to shreds. It was tragic. The General, with tears in his eyes, was stirring the boy's body.

Collingsworth and I looked down and wondered who packed the chute. That was all we could think about--who packed the chute that had the malfunction. I said, "General Gavin, I am Jack Hyles." (I forget the rank I had; I was private most of the time.) "I am Private Hyles, Parachute Maintenance Company. This is Private Collingsworth, sir. We want to know who packed the chute."

General Gavin reached down and picked up the parachute, opened the inside of the parachute case and took out the log book and said, "Men, the chute was packed a week ago and the name is--Collingsworth." And I saw that eighteen-year-old boy shriek like a man who has seen a corpse--and he had. I saw him tremble. Putting his hands over his face, he began to scream. He ran as fast as he could across the field screaming, "Oh! Oh! I wish I had been more careful! Oh, I wish I had been more careful!" I can hear him now, that shriek of the eighteen-year-old kid way in the night.

We went to the barracks. We tried to comfort him. But all he would scream was, "I wish I had been more careful! I wish I had been more careful! I wish I had been more careful!" I have thought a thousand times since then about that boy. He will go through life with that scar on his mind.

He didn't do his best.

Yet some of us are going to look at people burning in Hell and scream, "I wish I had been more careful!"

There are people in your neighborhood to whom God has given you the custody of their soul. Cry about it and weep over them. Weep while they are alive. Don't do like I did --wait until your daddy is dead and gone, then cry over him. Cry now, weep now, care now. "They that sow in tears shall reap in joy."

And may it be said in our towns, "Jack Hyles wept; Bill Rice wept; John Rice wept; Walt Handford wept; Mary wept," as Jesus wept.

3

Stay in Crete

"To Titus, mine own son after the common faith: Grace, mercy, and peace, from God the Father and the Lord Jesus Christ our Saviour. For this cause left I thee in Crete, that thou shouldest set in order the things that are wanting, and ordain elders in every city, as I had appointed thee."--Titus 1:4, 5.

"That the aged men be sober, grave, temperate, sound in faith, in charity, in patience. The aged women likewise, that they be in behaviour as becometh holiness, not false accusers, not given to much wine, teachers of good things; That they may teach the young women to be sober, to love their husbands, to love their children, To be discreet, chaste, keepers at home, good, obedient to their own husbands, that the word of God be not blasphemed. Young men likewise exhort to be sober minded. In all things shewing thyself a pattern of good works: in doctrine shewing uncorruptness, gravity, sincerity, Sound speech, that cannot be condemned; that he that is of the contrary part may be ashamed, having no evil thing to say of you."--Titus 2:2-8.

Paul is writing a letter to his young preacher boy. Now Titus was on an island called Crete, and he was discouraged.

Many preachers are here this morning. You understand a little about Titus then. All of us have been there. Titus got discouraged. The offering was down. The Sunday School wasn't going too good. The deacons were giving a little trouble. The people were complaining. The ladies were gossiping. The prayer meeting crowd was off. Folks were calling Titus a nut and a fool. It was a difficult situation. Titus had a desire to leave. These conditions caused Titus to write a letter to Paul and say, "Now, Brother Paul, I would like for you to find me another place."

I have some preacher boys, and I get more letters from those preacher boys, saying, "Brother Hyles, I believe my ministry has ended here. I think God is through with me here. I have been here two months now, and I think I have about finished my work. I have preached up all my sermons. Would you recommend me somewhere else?" Usually such letters are written on Monday morning or late Sunday night!

I think Titus was like that. He was writing Paul and saying, "Dear Brother Paul: I appreciate your recommending me down here at Crete. This was a good situation. The salary was good, but I am having it a little rough now, and if you don't mind, I wish you would recommend me somewhere else."

So Paul is writing back to Titus to explain that he cannot recommend him somewhere else, that he ought to stay in Crete in spite of the fact that Crete is a difficult place, a hard place to stay. Paul is writing to tell him that he ought to stay there and fight the battle for God.

Now many of you are in difficult places today. Dr. Rice, you would be interested in this. One dear brother came to the conference last year and he got iron in his blood and grit in his craw and went back to preach what he ought to preach. He started doing thus and so and standing for right and before long the associational missionary came down. He brought a lawyer with him and caused trouble. This preacher said, "I had to leave the church. And do you know what I did? I started preaching in a barn." I asked, "How is the ministry?" He answered, "Fine. God is blessing. I am to baptize eight next Sunday night."

That is what these conferences do. Anyway, you come to places like this after being discouraged at home, and you get encouraged. That is what this is for--to encourage us.

I was in the paratroopers in World War II. The very thought of my ever getting up in a plane and jumping scares the daylights out of me. I fly a great deal. When I get up in those planes 34,000 feet and look down, I say, "Man alive! How did I ever jump out of one of these things!" But I did--well, I was pushed out nineteen times! Do you know why I could jump? Because there were seventeen other fellows on the plane about to jump, too. And if they were in the same shape I was in, it wasn't too bad.

So it is good to go aside and find fellows who have it rough, too. I am sure that many, many of you today are in rough situations. You are having it difficult. You have cried many tears lately. The burdens have been heavy; the problems many.

That is the way it was with Titus. He was in Crete. He wanted to come back. So Paul wrote Titus a letter. "Titus, I left you in Crete for this cause, 'that thou shouldest set in order the things that are wanting, and ordain elders in every city.'"

Actually Paul, in the letter of Titus, is trying to explain why he wants Titus left in Crete. I think the key phrase, the key sentence, in Titus is, "For this cause left I thee in Crete." Then he goes on to explain what to do in Crete, what to preach to the old ladies and to the old men, and to the young ladies and young men. He explains what Titus ought to do in Crete and why he should stay there.

Now there are three things Paul told Titus in so many words about why he ought to stay in Crete. In the first place, Paul said, "Titus, you need Crete. You need Crete." In the second place, he said in so many words, "Titus, Crete needs you." In the third place, he was saying, "God needs you in Crete."

Titus Needs Crete

Notice, first, Paul said, "Titus, you need Crete. Now I know the going gets rough." We come to a meeting of preachers and we laugh, we play. But there are many heartaches and burdens; there are tears and broken hearts; there are nights of weeping and nights of loneliness. There are times, you preacher friends, when nobody understands. I mean there are going to be times (if there are not already times) when you are not right with God. But there are going to be times and there are times when nobody understands.

Even your own best people won't understand. They are for you. They say to you, "Now, Preacher, we think you are fine, but why do you do like you do? We get out of one mess, then in another. Why do you do like you do?"

You go home and your wife says, "Honey, I don't want to see folks against you. Can't you preach the same thing and not be quite so tough? Why do you have to be so mean?"

And your mother sometimes says, "Son, Mamma loves you and Mamma hates to see you unhappy. Mamma hates to see you suffer. Son, isn't there some way you could preach the same thing without making so many folks mad at you? I don't want folks to get mad at you. You are not as mean as everybody says you are. Now, Son, couldn't you just ease up a little bit?"

You come home and your wife doesn't understand; the kids can't figure you out; the dog won't wag his tail at you. There is nobody at all who approves and you wonder if it is worth it. So you write Dr. Rice a letter and say, "Dr. Rice, I think my ministry is over here. Would you pray about recommending me somewhere else?" Dr. Rice writes back, "Now you behave yourself, and you stay in Crete." Brother, you don't think it, but you need to stay in Crete because it is the best thing for you. It is best that you stay in Crete. You need it.

I have noticed that all great men have had times of brokenness. In Dr. Rice's biography we read where he had some times when it seemed like his ministry was gone. He had some times when it seemed like he faced a critical point in his ministry, it seemed like everything was gone--times of discouragement.

For example, Dr. George W. Truett had a time when his heart was broken. He shot one of his best friends accidentally on a hunting trip, which almost broke his heart. But that was the mellowing thing that made his ministry, made God's breath upon him.

Take Mr. Charles Spurgeon. Spurgeon left the Baptist Union of Great Britain and Ireland. The group voted to censure him. Only seven folks voted for him when he was censured officially. Of course, the same Baptist headquarters has his picture now in the vestibule, but they would still break his heart if he were alive today. He was voted out. He had heartbreak. Not only that, but in Surrey Music Gardens packed with thousands, someone cried "Fire" and in the stampede several folks were killed. It broke Spurgeon's heart. This matter of Crete, the difficult place, the hard place, the rough going, was one of the things God used to make Spurgeon what he was.

Charles G. Finney had his Crete. Finney's pastor was named Dr. Dale. Dr. Dale was a good fundamental man, but like so many good fundamental men today. Dr. Dale ordained Charles G. Finney. Finney came to the place in his life when Dr. Dale said, "I am ashamed I laid my hands on Charles Finney, ashamed he is my son in the ministry." It broke Finney's heart. It was his Crete, but it was one of the best things that ever happened to him.

Jonathan Edwards was pastor of a thriving church. When he preached against dancing and unconverted church membership, the leaders in the church got together and voted him out. It broke his heart. It seemed as if his Crete was more than he could stand; yet it was one of the things that made Jonathan Edwards.

Now, dear friends, if John Rice and Charles Spurgeon and

George Truett and Billy Sunday and Dwight Moody and Charles Finney and Jonathan Edwards needed their Crete, I think Jack Hyles needs his. We ought to do as my Mamma used to say, "Son, quit your crying and open your mouth and take your Black Draught like a big boy." Now it is all I ever took. Black Draught medicine, it was claimed, would cure anything--anything from falling hair to ingrowing toenails to ptomaine poisoning to lumbago. And Mamma served it on the wrong end of the spoon! Did you ever take Black Draught on the wrong end of a spoon?

I would say, "Mamma, I have a headache." "O.K., open your mouth, Son." It is the most awful tasting stuff I ever tasted. She would say, "Open your mouth, Son." And I would say, "Mamma, I don't want to." She would say, "Stand up and take your medicine like a big boy." I sat there with my lips puckered and my eyes rolling with tears and opened my mouth. I learned to take my Black Draught like a big boy. Now we are going to have to do the same thing today.

Some of you preachers will go home and whine and complain and yelp and cry and moan and groan because the deacons are trying to chase you off. Now you just sit up and take your medicine like a big boy. Behave yourself. Stay in Crete. You need to stay there. It will do more for you than all the good times, all the happy times, all the big times. You will pray more, care more, cry more, grow more, get more, and bless more in those times of sorrow, heartache, bereavement and seeming defeat than any other time in your life. So if you are facing some tough times today, you stay in Crete.

I was reading the other day of Ronald Creech, one of our good friends, in Durham, North Carolina. Ronald Creech has taken a real stand for God in his area. Some of the little lean Christians, maybe they are broadminded, decided they were going to get rid of Ronald. They tried, but Ronald can't be got rid of. He wouldn't leave.

What happened? A little group of folks sued him; now most of the people who followed him had to leave the church building and have services outside. The church was roaming the streets trying to find a place to meet. But they were having folks saved right along, and the power of God was there. Old Ronald was facing a battle, but I will guarantee you one thing: there will be a different Ronald Creech who comes out of this than went into it. Why? Because it is his Crete. And he needs it. Now the Court of Appeals has given the church back its building.

I was with a fellow down in West Memphis, Arkansas, who was in this conference last year. He went back home and stirred up some trouble. Listen! There is enough trouble to stir up at home. Well, you say, "I don't know what to preach against." Just look, man: there is enough meanness in your town. Preach a series of sermons on the meanness that is going on, and you will stir up some trouble. Listen. If you have the dancing out of the high school, work on the square dancing in the junior high school for a while. If you can get that out, work on the one-two-three-kick in the elementary schools. Do something, brother. There is enough meanness going on, enough devilment going on in your town for any prophet of God to keep in a scrap most of the time.

So this fellow left the conference and went back to West Memphis, Arkansas, and he had some of the wrong men down to preach in his church--I should say some of the right men. So he had to get excommunicated. He went and got him an old night club and converted the night club and is preaching there and now he is having about as many folks in the night club as he had down in the church building, and he doesn't have to be worried about the associational missionary.

I am just saying this: Difficult times when you can get in a scrap for God will make you if you will just stand up and fight. You need Crete.

I can say this for my own little ministry: In my life the biggest things that ever happened to me, happened in times of sorrow. One night Dad had just come home--many nights, but this one night in particular, Mamma and I waited for Daddy on Saturday night to come home but he didn't come. Finally about four o'clock in the morning we heard a noise down the street. Daddy had hit a tree. He had come in drunk, and had a flat, and didn't even know it, he was so drunk. He hit a tree and the car was ruined. Mamma's heart was broken. Daddy came in and Mamma talked and cried. She tiptoed out in the backyard and got a bottle of whiskey out of the car; I saw her break it on a rock in the backyard so Daddy wouldn't have any more.

I began to cry--a little kid of about ten or eleven years old, and I said, "Mamma, why can't Daddy go to Sunday School like other daddies?" My heart was crushed and broken. It seemed that Mamma and I just didn't know what in the world to do. But it wasn't but a few hours before God spoke to me about getting saved. Through that little experience I came to Christ.

Then one day when I was a teen-ager, I came home. Mother called me in the room and said, "Son, I have something to tell you."

I said, "What, Mother?"

"Daddy is leaving this morning."

Daddy was sitting on the bed, and I said, "Daddy, you are not going to leave."

Daddy said, "Yes, Son, it has got to be this way."

It was Sunday morning. I went to church that night brokenhearted. In that time God spoke to my heart about being a preacher.

God uses those sorrowful times, God uses the tears, God uses the Crete experiences, God uses the difficult times to work on you and get you right.

I thought the world had ended when I buried my father. I thought the sun would never rise. I thought that life was over. I complained to God. Yet whatever little success God has given me in the ministry and blessing in soul winning is because of what happened on the grave of my daddy.

Now let me tell you something, preachers: Quit giving up. I get tired of preachers giving up every time they have it rough. I get sick of some old backslidden, skinflint of a deacon coming to the preacher and saying, "We are going to try to chase you off." The preacher, too sweet for his own breeches, gets up and says, "Well, I guess I had better leave. I don't want to cause any trouble."

What do you mean--you don't want to cause any trouble? You cause him all the trouble you can. You chase that fellow so far they won't ever know who he was. You put him in orbit. I know what you will do. You will say, "Well, I don't want to cause any trouble. My wife is having heart trouble, the kids are getting complications, and I am getting a little ulcer myself. I just believe it would be better if I moved on and the church would have peace."

Yes, they will have peace. That fellow will run that just like he ran it while you were there, and he will kill somebody else's wife, and somebody else's kids, and ruin somebody else's family, and ruin somebody else's health. Don't you leave that fellow to ruin some other good man. You stay there and fight the battle, and don't leave until the battle is won. I mean, stay in your Crete and fight and do the job for God when it is hard; stay when it is tough; stay when it is rough; stay when they try to chase you off. In God's good name, stay.

Sure, you will have trouble. Sure, you will have rough going. Sure, they will try to chase you off. But don't fold your little wings and get out. Stay there and fight the battle for God. You need Crete. You need those experiences. You need it tough.

I wonder sometimes what we think Christianity is. Let me picture it a minute. Go to the city of Ephesus in the first century. Come to Corso Street, the street on which the big arena and the big athletic contests were held. See the great crowds and activity as fifty or sixty thousand or more people gather together for a great athletic contest. See them as they get off their chariots or camels and park them, tie them; see them as they walk down toward the great stands of the great arena. See them as the men of the concession stands try to sell their refreshments. Great crowds are coming in and thousands of people are in the great arena on Corso Street in Ephesus.

See them as the mayor of the city and the city councilmen gather in the press box high above the stadium. See them as the people gather in the city of Ephesus for the great athletic contest and as they start the contest and have someone throw the javelin, and the great javelin contest gets under way.

There are a few races and a discus throw, etc., and after a few preliminaries, now you come to the main event. And the crowd will scream, "Bring on all the Christians! Bring on the Christians!"

Over in the corner somewhere is a little huddle of God's people, redeemed by Calvary's blood, saved by His marvelous grace, who love not their lives unto death. They are huddled in a little corner. Down here on this end of the arena is a cage. In that cage there are several big ravenous lions who have not had one bite of food for an entire week. Their cage is down here on this end. The crowd begins to chant just like you would chant, "We want a touchdown! We want a touchdown! Or block that kick! Block that kick! Or we want a home run!" Then comes the great chant, the main event, "Bring on the Christians! Bring on the Christians! Bring on the Christians!"

Down here on this end are the lions; someone opens the door and they push them in. Among that little huddle of Christians is a tottering gray-haired man, a dear grandmotherly saint, a young man, a young lady expecting a baby, a few little children--not very important-looking people, not very well dressed, not very stately, not very influential, not very wealthy. They come into the arena and as they look at the great crowd they realize what is going to happen. Somebody pulls a rope and the lions, who have been starved for seven days, are turned loose. The lions come toward the Christians and have their breakfast. In a little huddle the Christians begin to pray and sing:

Amazing grace! how sweet the sound,
That saved a wretch like me!
I once was lost, but now am found,
Was blind, but now I see.

Thro' many dangers, toils and snares,
I have already come;
'Tis grace hath bro't me safe thus far,
And grace will lead me home.

Those little Christians in Ephesus in the first century bowed together in a little circle on their knees in prayer as the lions came and as the people roared with delight and joy, "Kill the Christians! Kill the Christians!" Death came as the lions ripped their bodies to pieces and broke their bones into powder. The few Christians died for Jesus Christ.

That is where this thing we are in started, dear friends. Early Christianity was a religion of martyrs. Yet we groan today. We think the preacher has to be chaplain of the local Masonic Lodge; he has to be the blesser of the Civic Clubs, the trigger-puller every time there is a turtle race in town. He is somewhat of a cross between grandmother, Santa Claus and Old Mother Hubbard. He is a holy water blesser. He walks down the street with his sweet little smile all week long and blesses the people, and folks say, "There goes the Reverend, boys and girls. Grow up and be like him. He is a sweet, kindly man who never says anything negative. He never raises his voice or lets his temper go."

Yes, and lets the whole world go to Hell. He doesn't tell anybody about sin. He lets the night clubs run rampant. He lets the boys and girls go into adultery. He lets the town go to Hell. He lets the skid rowers go on their mad plunge t ward Hell. He lets broken homes continue and broken liv and broken hearts and broken futures and broken dreams down the cesspool of his own indifference and cowarc preaching. "Let them go to Hell," he says. "I am saved.

Somewhere between the first century and 1961 we ha' definitely lost the thing that made Christianity what it wa and the thing that Jesus intended for His people to be and l like. God help us to realize we have not been called to Sunday School picnic, but to fight a battle for God. Y(need to stay in Crete and fight the battle.

You are not going to see any Red Seas parted until tl Pharaohs get after you. Everybody wants to see the R(Sea parted, but nobody wants the Pharaohs chasing them.

Everybody wants to see the Son of man standing at tl right hand of God, but nobody wants to get stoned as Steph(was.

Everybody wants to go to the third Heaven, but nobo(wants to get chased out of Lystra as Paul did.

Everybody wants to see Leo the lion get lockjaw, but nc body wants to bow and pray with the windows open and g(with Daniel into the lions' den.

Everybody wants to see Jesus standing in the fiery fur nace, but nobody wants to refuse to bow down and worshi the golden image and get put in the fiery furnace.

Everybody wants to see God's blessing and powe Everybody wants to see revival. "Lord, send a pentecosta revival." Yes, if God did send a pentecostal revival yo would be put in jail as were Peter and John; they would ston you as they did Stephen; they would laugh at you as they di Peter. They would mock you and persecute you and haur you. I am saying that not a single preacher in this buildin today but what does not need a good old tough, scrappin battle such as Crete to make a man out of you. You nee Crete. Titus needed Crete.

Crete Needs Titus

In the second place, not only does Titus need Crete, but Crete needs Titus. "Paul, could I go home? Paul, it is cold and lonely. Paul, you yourself said they were a bunch of slow bellies. And Paul, among these slow bellies over here --it is hard, rough. Paul, could I go somewhere else? Could I move on to a more lucrative field? I feel my work is done here."

Paul said, "Titus, you stay in Crete not only because you need Crete, but because Crete needs you."

Fellows, listen today. Neighborhoods around this country by the thousands have no gospel witness whatsoever. People write me by the hundreds who hear me on the radio station and say, "Brother Hyles, we don't have any place to go to church." "Brother Hyles, do you know of a soul-winning church near enough to us where we could go? We live in Montana. We live in Washington, D. C. We live in New Jersey. We live in Texas. We live in Oklahoma. We live in Georgia. We live in Idaho. We live in Michigan. We live in Indiana. Brother Hyles, we don't know a soul-winning church where we can go." Ah, places across this country need preachers.

Old Dr. Scarborough used to say down at Southwestern Seminary as he looked out at his class of preachers, "Young men, be resurrection preachers." They would look bewildered. And Dr. Scarborough would say, "Go after these old dead churches and resurrect them. Set them on fire for God. Give these neighborhoods a place to go to church."

"Listen, Crete needs some young preachers today. Crete needs some young men who are aflame for God, who are afraid of nobody but God, seek nothing but souls, love nothing but God's will, hate nothing but sin, fight nothing but the Devil. John Wesley used to say, "We will go out to these towns and start new churches."

My little girl, Becky, is nine. My little girl, Linda, is almost four. David is seven. My little Cindy is twenty months old. David is going to be a preacher, I think. He was going to be an ice cream man, but I have about talked him into being a preacher now! I asked him the other day, "David, what are you going to be?" He said, "Preacher."

David and Becky got to the office the other day. They turned on the recording machine. I don't know how, but they turned it on, and David and Becky were having a service. I played it back after they were gone. Boy, it was a lark! It was almost sacrilegious. If they weren't so young it would be a sin.

David said, "Well everybody, we are glad to see this big crowd. Would you all stand and sing and shake hands and get acquainted?"

Becky said, "Amen! Glory to God!"

David said, "Now then, do we have any visitors here?"

Becky answered, "I am one."

He said, "Where are you from, young lady?"

"I am from Texas."

He said, "We are glad to have you. Amen."

"Amen," she said.

Then he said, "Now we are going to sing a solo."

He got up and brother, he warbled it! He tremoloed it. He sang, "Amazing Grace...!" Boy he really hatched it up. When he got through he said, "Now I am going to preach." You talk about preaching! I never heard such preaching. That old recording machine just shook! He said, "If you don't get borned again, you are going to burn forever and ever in Hell where there is fire and it is hot fire, too."

And Becky said, "Hallelujah! Amen! Glory to God!"

Then he said, "Now all you heathen bow your heads. We are going to have an invitation. If you want to get saved, come on down here."

Old Becky said, "I am coming." She came down.

And he said, "Do you want to get saved?"

"Yes sir."

He said, "Kneel there and pray it through."

"O. K." And she prayed and he said, "O Lord, help this dear old sinner woman to get saved."

She said, "Hallelujah! I am saved now!"

David said, "Are you sure you are saved?"

"Yes sir, I am sure."

He said, "Folks, this lady just got saved."

Becky said, "Glory to God!"

Boy, it was terrible, it really was. I saw myself finally as others see me. Now I wonder where he got that?

But you know Becky, Cindy, Linda and David are not going to be at home forever. One of these days Becky is going to marry some fellow and go off to Seattle, or San Francisco, or Portland, or Washington, or Norfolk, or Winston-Salem, or Miami, or Orlando, or Birmingham, or Atlanta, where her husband will get a job. I hope there is a good church where she can go. I hope that in the little town where they settle there will be a gospel-preaching, soul-winning, Hell-defeating, Christ-honoring, sin-fighting church. And I hope she will be able to see somebody saved every Sunday. My little girl Becky, nine years old, almost ten, has never been to church on Sunday without seeing somebody saved. Not one of my children has ever been to church on Sunday without seeing somebody saved. I hate to think that Becky would have to rear her family in some old cold, dead church.

But what are we going to do? How are we going to get them? I know how we are going to get them. When fellows like you go back home and tell your deacons you are going to preach what God tells you to preach. Tell them by God's grace you are going to preach what God says to preach and build some soul-winning stations. Get off your blessed assurance, out of your luxurious office, and get out here on the street corner and knock on doors and go from house to house and tell folks about Jesus and get them saved and bring them down the aisle on Sunday and build the saints in the faith and preach the Bible and stand for God. If we could raise a generation of young preachers around this country like that, we would have a station in every town in America where the truth is preached and souls get saved. So Crete needs Titus.

One fellow said to me, "Brother Hyles, if God should call me up North of the Mason-Dixon line, I just am not interested." I guess I am an ambassador for the North now, but some of you fellows who are down here where there are good churches on every street corner, did you ever stop to think that there are towns of thousands of people in America that don't have a single church that believes the Bible is the Word of God? Did you know there are cities with twenty-five and thirty and forty thousand people that don't have one single soul-winning witness in town? I am just saying this: Because it is hard does not give you a right to fold up and quit. Stay in the battle. Crete needs you. That hard place needs you.

Let me say this, too: Don't let Crete change you; you change Crete. I have been in Crete. I have had tough things, but I haven't had any bad things. Nobody has yet crucified me, nobody has spit at me yet. Oh, I may have been spit at, but I ducked! But we have been in a few places that were rougher than we are used to.

Listen to me now. When you get to these tough places, just say, "Dear Lord, by God's grace I need it, I can take it. I will fight it because I need it." And Crete also needs you.

Look what Paul told Titus to preach. In chapter 2, verse 2, he said, tell "the aged men be sober [that means don't drink], grave [that means don't tell dirty stories], temperate [that means don't eat too much], sound in the faith [that means fight liberalism, modernism, neo-orthodoxy and all the rest of it], in charity [that means teach them to love God, love Him enough to serve Him], in patience [that means to keep on serving God when the going is rough]."

And he said tell the old women, this means the W. M. S.,

tell the "aged women likewise, that they be in behaviour as becometh holiness [tell them to straighten up and live clean], not false accusers [tell them to use their tongue right and quit yakking], not given to much wine [tell them to quit going to their social clubs and their civic parties and drinking their little cocktails, their canasta clubs], teachers of good things." And he says, "Teach the young women to be sober, to love their husbands, to love their children, to be discreet, chaste, keepers at home, good, obedient to their own husbands, that the word of God be not blasphemed."

"Young men likewise exhort to be sober minded." That means to be careful what you read. Keep your mind clean. Quit looking at naked women, and women, you quit going naked. "In all things shewing thyself a pattern of good works: in doctrine shewing uncorruptness, gravity, sincerity, Sound speech [quit your cursing, dirty jokes, lying, all of your bad talking] ...."

Now he said, "That is what I left you there for." He said, "You have a bunch of slow bellies over there." He said, "Tell the old men to straighten up. Get the old ladies to quit gossiping. Get the young ladies to keep the houses and to quit working downtown to make a little more money. Tell them to wear enough clothes. Tell the young men to keep their minds clean and pure." He said, "The meaner they are, the more they need you."

Anybody can go to a place where all the Christians are doing real good and make it fine. I had a church in Texas with three hundred soul winners, 4,128 members when I left. I never saw a bunch of folks in my life who loved God any more. We had several people who won souls every week and some won folks every day. One man won over two hundred a year. Two or three folks won 150 people a year to Christ. Over three hundred won somebody in a year. Twenty-five or more won somebody every week. Boy, you could come to our church and say, "Jesus saves," and folks would shout "Amen!" I mean it was just an utopian situation. Anybody can serve God like that.

When the going gets rough, when the deacons breathe down your throat, when people are living in sin and they want to chase the preacher off, if you cut loose on this matter of sin and if you teach the boys and girls they ought to live right and dress right and act right and be good witnesses at school; and you teach the men they ought to take down those dirty calendars and quit reading that sexy literature and keep their minds clean; and you teach the young ladies they ought to dress right and walk right and sit right and live right and drink right and lead right; and you teach the old men they ought to come to church and be examples; and teach these old ladies to quit gossiping and get right with God; and just because you have a gray hair in your head it doesn't give you an exemption from visitation and witnessing and soul winning--when you bear down on that thing, you may as well make up your mind that a committee will see you within thirty days. You just get ready for them. Put the coffee pot on and make some doughnuts; they are on the way to see you!

Paul said, "Titus, I am not saying to ease up; I am saying to speed it up and fight the battle for God."

I asked my little boy, "What are you going to be when you grow up?"

"A preacher."

"Are you going to be a real good, hard-hitting, sin-fighting, Hell-hating, Christ-honoring, soul-winning preacher, or a pussyfooter."

He answered, "I am going to be a pussyfooter."

Sometimes I don't blame him.

Paul said to Titus, "Crete needs you." Listen, dear friends, if you don't change your town, there is no use in your being in your town.

Dr. John Rice down in Waxahachie, Texas, twenty miles north from where I was born, was in a revival campaign.

Many of the young folks were going out to lover's lane. Dr. Rice one night announced, "I am going out to lover's lane tonight after the service and take down the car license of every car out there, then tomorrow night in this mule barn I will read off the number of the car license of everybody in lover's lane tonight." That would cause a stir wouldn't it?

Where is that old stuff today? Oh, we garnish their tombstones. We say about Billy Sunday, "Let's garnish his tombstone. God bless the memory of Billy Sunday, that wonderful preacher of the Gospel. Oh, God give us more Billy Sundays." Well, why don't you preach like Billy Sunday did? If we are going to brag on Billy Sunday, let's do the best we can to try to encourage Billy Sunday-type Christianity. Ma Sunday told me before she died, "Jack, when Billy preached he didn't have an outline; he had a sign board with figures an inch high. The reason was that he didn't get close to the pulpit, so he couldn't see his little outline. He ran by the pulpit every once in a while, and he had to have a sign instead of an outline." Yes, we garnish their tombstones.

Dr. Rice doesn't think he is as old as I sometimes make it sound like he is. I don't think he is real old either. I think he is a young man, but he is not twenty anymore. He is not twenty-nine anymore. But he won't be dead five years before some of these little fellows who won't even speak to him on the street will be preaching a series of sermons out of his books and talking about "the great John Rice."

Dear friends, do you know what we need? We don't need some fellows who like Billy Sunday; we need some little Billy Sundays scattered all over the country. We don't need some fellows to talk about the great Moody; we need some fellows who will act like the great Moody where they live. So Crete needed Titus.

God Needs You in Crete

The next thing very quickly and that is, God needs you in

Crete. The writer Ezekiel said there was nobody to "stand in the gap" (Ezek. 22:30).

The psalmist said, "I looked on my right hand...refuge failed; no man cared for my soul" (Ps. 142:4).

God needs you in Crete. God needs somebody in Crete. Let me say this: If you will stay after sinners and be faithful to God, God can use you in Crete. It would be a good thing today if some preachers here could go home and get kicked out of your churches for Jesus. I am not saying you ought to try to; I am not saying you ought to; but I am saying some of you ought to, if you got kicked out for Jesus.

I was in the 82nd Airborne Division, stationed at Fort Bragg, North Carolina, but I never saw combat duty. But some of the fellows who did, came back from overseas and showed their wounds. One fellow would say, "Well, I have a plate in my head. I got it in Okinawa." Another fellow would say, "I got some shrapnel in my leg and it is still there. I got that in Iwo Jima." Another fellow would say, "Well, see this empty sleeve? I lost my arm over in the Belgian Bulge." One fellow would say, "I have got an imitation foot or a wooden leg. I lost my leg in Normandy."

They would look at me as if to say, "Well, how about you?" I would say, "I got dish pan hands on K. P. while you all were over there." Sometimes I wished I could have a broken leg. I got to where I wished I could have a piece of shrapnel or a plate in my skull, or an artificial limb or something because I was so embarrassed.

Now won't we little 4F Christians who let sin run wild and loose in our town be ashamed when we stand before Jesus? Paul will say, "I bear in my body the marks of the Lord Jesus Christ. I got these old lumps down there at Lystra. How about you, Stephen?" Old Stephen will say, "Well, I got stoned outside the city. I too got a few lumps for Jesus." How about you, John? "Well, I was out there a long time; I was awfully lonely on the isle of Patmos." James will say, "I was beheaded." Philip will say, "I was crucified." Matthew will say, "I was clubbed to death." James the less will say, "My brains were beaten out." Andrew will say, "I was crucified with two of the poles sticking in the ground diagonally." Mark will say, "I was dragged to pieces." Paul will say, "I was beheaded." Jude and Bartholomew will say, "I was crucified." Thomas will say, "I was killed with a spear." Luke will say, "I was hanged." John will say, "I was a fanatic and exiled." We little old twentieth century preachers will say, "All we have is a little mimeograph ink on our hands when we put out the bulletin every Saturday morning." Ah, God give us some preachers again!

Wouldn't it be a good thing if every little child could be raised to listen to a preacher who loved God and loved sinners and got them saved?

Wouldn't it be a good thing if once again the boys and girls in our country could hear the old-time preaching that some of you used to hear? I go to preach in places nowadays and folks say, "I used to hear that when I was a kid." Now when our kids grow up they will have to say, "I never heard that. I never heard that." And the reason is that there is just not much preaching going on today--the right kind of preaching.

When I was a kid they used to ask, "Where are you going, Jack?" "I am going to preaching." But now they say, "I am going to church." Why? There is no preaching. They used to say, "How many boys and girls are going to attend preaching today?" Now they say, "How many of you boys and girls are going to attend church today?" Why? The preaching is gone. The churches are building great big educational buildings to house a thousand, and an auditorium to take care of three hundred. Why? Preaching is gone.

I am saying, God needs some preachers to go to Crete. When Charles G. Finney was in Rochester in a revival the school principal got mad at him. The teacher tried to run him down, criticize him and cuss him. And Charles G. Finney was praying and the power of God fell. One day a boy was in the high school giving a talk and he fell under conviction and got on his face and began to weep and confess his sins. When that happened, the entire class began to weep and confess their sins. The principal was called in and the teacher said, "What are we going to do?" And the principal said, "I don't know what to do. What can we do?" And the teacher said, "Well, I don't know." The principal said, "Go call that preacher. He is the only one who can help us." And he did. The revival broke out in school. Isn't that wonderful? Now compare that with our baccalaureate sermons today.

As you look back at those difficult days, you will find the sweetest times of all were the years you spent in Crete. Titus looks back from Heaven today and I am sure Titus can say, "Crete was the best place I ever was in. I needed it. The people needed me and God needed me in Crete."

When I left Texas and went to Hammond, it was the hardest thing I ever did. I mean it was the hardest thing I ever did in my life. I had a church of people who were my babies, my little children. In almost seven years, we had seen the church grow from a building worth six thousand dollars to over half a million dollars. We had seen the church grow from forty-four members to over four thousand. They were my babies. I loved them just like I love my own flesh.

Before my wife and I left Garland, I was supposed to preach my closing sermon on Sunday night. I couldn't do it. I left town that afternoon. I didn't even go back. I still owe them a sermon! When I got to the city limit sign I couldn't see the road. I began to cry. When we saw the sign, "Garland, Texas," both my wife and I began to weep. I stopped the car, turned around in the middle of the road and started back. My wife said, "What are you going to do?" I said, "I am going to go back. I am not going to Hammond."

She said, "But the Lord led us there." I said, "I don't care. I am going back. I am not going." We cried. We turned around and stopped and I said, "Sweetheart, I think I will go into evangelism. (The church had already called a pastor). You can live in Garland and I will preach in revivals. We can still live in the same place and have our old friends and see our converts." We cried some more sitting there in the car. But realizing God was leading us, we took off again for Hammond.

When I got to Hammond I walked into the auditorium and sat down in the seat on the platform. It didn't fit, Dr. Rice. The seat didn't even fit. I was used to sitting in a chair about like these over here. Our auditorium in Texas was just plain as vanilla. We have four walls and a roof, and as long as we stayed dry and warm we didn't care what we had. I sat down. I felt like a king who had just walked up on his throne. I mean it just didn't fit.

Looking behind me I saw a pipe organ. I had never pastored a church with one. And the building was high, with a big dome. Way up at the top was a sign, "God is light." But there wasn't enough light in the building. It was dark in the building.

I went into the office. It was big and didn't fit. I made a garage into an office and that is where my office was in Texas. The office was pretty and had this glass brick and imitation flowers, a big desk and everything. But when I sat down it just didn't fit. The seat didn't fit, the desk didn't fit, the auditorium didn't fit, the chair didn't fit. I got in the pulpit and it didn't fit. So I sat down and cried. And I said to myself: What does a fellow do the first day he is pastor of the First Baptist Church of Hammond, Indiana? I don't have anything to do. Here I am--with a church and nothing to do.

I reached in the drawer where there were some cards. I picked them up and found they were prospects. I took off and went visiting. As I knocked at a door a very refined lady came to the door, a lady in her middle fifties. I said, "How do you do? My name is Hyles."

And she told me her name.

She said, "What part of the South are you from?"

I said, "I am from Texas, and I just got here and I am homesick, but I want to tell you about Jesus."

She said, "I am very busy and I must go, I must leave. I don't have time."

I said, "Could you just let me tell you about Jesus?"

She said, "Well, go ahead but I have to hurry. I can't take much time to listen."

I told her about Jesus. I was on the outside but I had my hand on the screen door. As I told her about Jesus, I said, "Could I pray before I leave?"

She said, "You must hurry. I must go."

I cried and prayed and as I prayed a warm tear hit my right hand. My eyes were shut. I was crying, but I knew tears couldn't go out that way, and I knew it wasn't mine, and there wasn't anybody there but me and her. And so I gathered it must be her tears. Man alive! That was the sweetest tear I ever felt in my life! She prayed and came to Christ. Later she was baptized.

I went back down to the church and walked into the auditorium. It was bright and light as you can imagine. I sat down in the chair and the chair was a perfect fit! I got behind the pulpit, and it was made to order! Those organ pipes were the prettiest things I had ever seen in my life! I went in my office and it looked like a garage made into an office! I sat down at the desk and the chair was so comfortable, and the desk just fit! Why? Because I was doing the thing that God had called me to do.

Whether in Hammond, or in Garland, or in Tennessee, the thing God has called me and you to do is to get people saved. And when we do it, everything fits.

You see, if it is rough going where you are today, you need it, and they need you, and God needs you there.

4

Seeing Him Who Is Invisible

"Who through faith subdued kingdoms, wrought righteousness, obtained promises, stopped the mouths of lions, Quenched the violence of fire, escaped the edge of the sword, out of weakness were made strong, waxed valiant in fight, turned to flight the armies of the aliens. Women received their dead raised to life again: and others were tortured, not accepting deliverance that they might obtain a better resurrection: And others had trial of cruel mockings and scourgings, yea, moreover of bonds and imprisonment: They were stoned, they were sawn asunder, were tempted, were slain with the sword: they wandered about in sheepskins and goatskins; being destitute, afflicted, tormented; (Of whom the world was not worthy:) they wandered in deserts, and in mountains, and in dens and caves of the earth. And these all, having obtained a good report through faith, received not the promise: God having provided some better thing for us, that they without us should not be made perfect." --Heb. 11:33-40.

Now turn back, if you will, to verse 24 of Hebrews 11, then carefully follow in the reading of verses 24 to 27.

"By faith Moses, when he was come to years, refused to be called the son of Pharaoh's daughter; Choosing rather to suffer affliction with the

> people of God, than to enjoy the pleasures of sin for a season; Esteeming the reproach of Christ greater riches than the treasures in Egypt: for he had respect unto the recompence of the reward. By faith he forsook Egypt, not fearing the wrath of the king: for he endured [notice very carefully the next line], AS SEEING HIM WHO IS INVISIBLE."

Now brethren, let's face it. We are in the fight of our lives. It has been made exceedingly difficult in my town. For six or seven years I have been standing in my town and fighting Norman Vincent Pealism, National Council of Churchism and all the rest of it, and my folks believed what I said. Now there come those who preach the same message that I preach, yet embrace those whose doctrine I have fought through the years. My people come to me and ask me the same questions your people ask you: "Brother Hyles, we have always thought Norman Vincent Peale taught a doctrine that is wrong and lacked the punch. And we have always thought it was wrong to affiliate with the National Council. We have always thought it was wrong to associate with World Council people, and yet, Brother Hyles, there are people today who preach basically the same message that you preach who associate with those people."

I lose people from my church, and many of you do--people who can't understand. They feel perhaps through the years we've been too narrow, our message has been too biased, and we have been a little prejudiced against some people and jealous and what not, because we have preached through the years some basic fundamental things. Now those who preach basically the same message we preach embrace those who formerly were our enemies. Black used to be black and white white; but now it has become a dirty gray till a person can hardly tell what is black and what is white.

Now brethren, how are we going to take these things?

I don't know about you, but I get discouraged sometimes. Sometimes I think nobody is left but me.

I say to my wife, "How did you like my sermon?" With her tongue in cheek she says, "Good." I know what she means. And the dog won't wag his tail at me; the cat won't even come and let me feed him milk. It seems as though the whole world is down on me. I can walk under the door without bending over. I can sit in the gutter and dangle my feet. It seems nothing is going right. I get discouraged, and so do you. Many times you, like me, shed tears of loneliness and sorrow.

Sometimes I wish some preacher with convictions would come to my town with whom I could agree. I wish he would come to be pastor in my town so my own folks wouldn't think I was the only one in the world who was against something. It seems everything that goes on I have to get against. I get out of one scrap right into another. I don't mean to fight. Really I like people and want to get along with them; yet it seems there is one scrap after another.

So I get discouraged. You laugh now, but you are laughing because you were crying yesterday! When two people get together who have tuberculosis, and they cough, your cough doesn't sound so loud if somebody else is coughing along with you! We get discouraged and down in the dumps and wonder if it is worth it all.

You think the battle is raging now--it has just begun. The same Devil that fought yesterday is alive today. The same Devil that put these Christians into lions' mouths and in flames of fire is still alive today. Are we going to take it?

Look at Moses. Moses chose to serve God rather than all the riches of Egypt. Moses, how did you take it?

"I've seen Him who is invisible."

You are not going to take it unless every once in awhile you get a glimpse of Him who is invisible.

Aren't you tired of just going to church? Aren't you tired of singing the "Doxology" and "How Tedious and Tasteless the Hours" and "How Dry I Am"? The preacher does the best he can; he tries to get in touch with Heaven, but the line is busy. The operator is off for the week-end and you can't get through. Aren't you tired of going to church, then going home and feeling you haven't heard from Heaven? But when we go to church and God comes and talks to us and we feel His presence, then we go home and feel so good!

There are times when I go to church--it's one of those mornings we slept a little later and I had to dress all three kids by myself. Just about the time we are ready to leave, we discover Linda Lou's right shoe is on her left foot and her left shoe on her right foot. We get in the car and David wants a drink--got to go back and get him a drink. We go to church and Becky feels that she doesn't look just right, and my wife's dress is wrinkled because the baby wallowed all over her. I get up in the pulpit and try to get in touch with Heaven but can't. I go home and realize I have failed.

Brother, when your people come to hear you preach, they come to hear from Heaven. And if you fail to give them something straight off the altar from Heaven, you ought to resign your pulpit and let somebody in there who can get a call through to Heaven. Now you had as well face this. You will kill yourself if you don't see Him who is invisible every once in awhile.

In the last year I have been voted out of everything. I got voted out of the Dallas County Baptist Association on October 19, 1957. It's funny now; it was sad then. Do you know what October 10 is in the Bible? The Day of Atonement! (Both Joe Boyd and I were voted out the same time.) The Day of Atonement was the day the high priest took two goats. Do you recall the offering of the scapegoat? On that day the high priest took two goats. He killed one of them and left the other out in the wilderness and said, "Don't you ever come back." Now that happened to me.

Oh, I don't want to preach if I can't get in touch with Him who is invisible. I don't want fellowship with God's people if I can't have God's fellowship. The reason you are at this conference is because you want to see Him who is invisible. If you go home from this conference after hearing these men but have not had fellowship with and seen Him who is invisible, you have cheated yourself out of $20, or whatever you spent to get here.

There are three basic things about people who see Him who is invisible. Moses saw Him in the burning bush. Saul saw Him on the Damascus Road. Stephen saw Him when he was being stoned to death. Paul saw Him when he was outside the city of Lystra. The Hebrew children saw Him in the fiery furnace. Jacob saw him wrestling at midnight. Daniel saw Him in the lions' den. And others saw Him. And if you want to see Him, you will have to have these three basic things these men had.

Only in Heartbreak, Perhaps, Will You See Him Who Is Invisible

Every man in the Bible who saw Him who is invisible was a man of heartache. He was a man of loneliness. He was a man who bore reproach. These three things accompanied those in the Bible who saw Him who is invisible.

Brethren, the times when I have seen Him who is invisible were those times when my heart was broken. Those were good times. It seems the Lord has a wonderful way of turning adversity into victory. It seems He has a wonderful way of turning heartache into victory, and times of loneliness and despair into victory. Preacher brethren, isn't it good when you get in the middle of the battle and get discouraged and down in the dumps, to know that God really called you to preach?

I recall several experiences in my life when I have seen Him who is invisible. There are times when I get lonely, discouraged, down in the dumps. In those times it seems God has given me a vision of Him who is invisible.

My first experience took place when I was a small boy. I promised God on my daddy's grave that everywhere I would tell this experience. My daddy was a drunkard. I was raised in a poor home with no conveniences--just a little cabin on the edge of town. Because she couldn't afford a dress to wear to walk across the platform, my sister couldn't get her diploma with the rest of her class.

It came time for me to graduate. The morning of the commencement exercise, I had nothing but a pair of blue jeans and a tee shirt to wear to my own graduation. I looked in the closet and said, "O God, give me something to wear to commencement tonight. I can't wear blue jeans and a tee shirt." When I went to the mailbox at noon there was a $50 check from one of my old uncles. He wrote, "Spend it for your graduation present." I went downtown, bought a suit and graduated with as pretty a suit as anybody had.

I was raised poor. My little old mother--God bless her--had a life full of heartaches. Her daddy was mean and beat her; he didn't love her as he ought to. She married a drunkard at seventeen and had a little baby girl when she was eighteen. This baby was born an invalid, never walked or talked. When she was seven she died. My mother had another little girl and at seven she died.

I shall never forget one night. My dad didn't come home. He was out drunk. We had nothing to eat, so Mamma came to me and said, "Son, let's go to bed early tonight." I thought, "Well...okay." Then I heard Mamma crying. I didn't know then why, but now I realize it was because there was nothing to eat, and no wood to put in the stove. About four o'clock in the morning I heard Mother open the door. Daddy came stumbling in. The car was torn up; he was broke and bloody. There wasn't anything worth living for, it seemed.

I can recall wishing Daddy would go to church. It was Saturday night. I can recall going over as a little boy and getting on my knees and looking up and saying, "Daddy, why don't you go to church tomorrow?" Daddy would shove me away and say, "I don't have time for church."

Somehow God spoke to my heart that day and I went to church. That night I saw Him who is invisible. I got saved that night.

So you know God gives us experiences with Him who is invisible through heartaches and tragedy.

When I became a teen-ager I saw my daddy leave home, and Mother and I had to rough it the best we could. I went to work and tried to take care of Mother as she had taken care of me. I still try to take care of her. Even to this day I still pay my mother's rent and take care of the food. She is a member of my church now, is seventy-odd-years-old, and I get to preach to her every Sunday. She thinks I'm better than John Rice!

I went to work to take care of Mother, but it seemed we couldn't make ends meet, couldn't pay the bills. One day I went to church so forsaken and so forlorn--I just didn't know what to do. You know what the Lord did? God called me to preach that day! I saw Him who is invisible.

So in every deep experience I have ever had, I had to cry before I laughed. You have to go down before you can go up; have to get sad before you get happy.

Loneliness, the Price of Seeing Him Who Is Invisible

Then I went through other experiences. When my daddy passed away I stood on his grave and asked God why. From that day to this I have not been the same man. God gave me a vision of Him who is invisible.

I wasn't going to say anything here about getting voted out of the Association, but I almost have to. You've heard about the Lone Ranger and Tonto. Tonto is the Indian companion of the Lone Ranger. They went out in the desert in Texas. Ten thousand Indians came toward them and attacked them from the north, and so they took off south. Then ten thousand Indians came from the south, and so they took off east. Then ten thousand Indians came from the east, so they took off west. Then ten thousand Indians came from the west. There were the Lone Ranger and Tonto, his Indian companion, out in the middle of forty thousand Indians, no way to go. They were coming down upon them quickly. The Lone Ranger looked at Tonto and said, "Tonto, what are we going to do?" Tonto looked at him and said, "Ugh, what do you mean 'we,' white man?"

That's what they said! When I was voted out of the Association, I had lots of friends [I thought they were friends]; so I went to them and said, 'What are we going to do?" They said, "Ugh, what do you mean 'we,' Jack?" There we were. Friends gone, revivals cancelled. The first day after it happened four speaking engagements were cancelled. A revivalist was coming to my church. Within two or three weeks he had cancelled our revival. It just seemed like the whole world had fallen in.

Actually, our people never even heard of the Association. They didn't know there was a Dallas Baptist Association. We belonged to it, but our folks didn't know it. They thought we had lost our charter. They thought we couldn't have services anymore. Lots of them said, "What are we going to do with the building now that we can't have a church anymore?" They thought that. Finally it dawned upon us what had happened, and for awhile we felt lonely.

I had been to a Southern Baptist college and seminary and pastored four Southern Baptist churches, and for awhile it seemed lonely. People we never dreamed would leave us, left us. Folks we never dreamed would break their friendship, broke their friendship. I mean the best friends I had, I thought, turned their backs on our church and upon me just like that.

Preacher boys whom God had saved and called to preach under our ministry, and everything they knew had been taught from our pulpit, left us just in a moment. They were gone. It seemed like the church was rocking and reeling. It seemed for awhile as if the whole thing was breaking in.

I said, "Lord, I'm going to leave. I feel led to be an evangelist. I'm going to leave." So I decided to go.

One night I was sound asleep, just enjoying a good night's rest. (I love to dream. I pray to God every night when I go to sleep, "Lord, let me dream something tonight. I don't want to waste my time while sleeping. Let me dream something tonight." I love to dream. Listen! I've been to Shanghai, China; I've been to Rome, Italy; I've been to London, England; I've preached city-wide revivals in New York City and Chicago; and I've never been to any of them. I did it in a dream. Wonderful experiences! I have seen literally thousands of people saved in my dreams. I love it! It's wonderful. You ought to get in the habit. Eat a hamburger before you go to bed every night and ask God to help you dream! God will do it!)

So I was sound asleep and dreaming. The telephone rang, and oh, the horror of a preacher's telephone at two o'clock in the morning! I thought, "I wonder who is dead now." I went to the phone and picked up the receiver. One of my custodians said, "Brother Jack, come to the church quickly."

"What in the name of common sense happened?"

"A tornado hit the educational building."

"Oh, no! Oh, no, no! A thousand times no. I'm still dreaming."

He said, "You're not dreaming. A tornado hit the educational building. Come quickly."

It was pouring down rain. Hail was on the ground. I rushed down to the churchhouse in the midst of the pouring down rain and hail, looked up and saw through the top of our educational building. The top story was blown off and was down against one of the other buildings. The water was going through and you could swim in the bottom floor. Furniture was broken. I looked at my associate pastor, who went with me--we lived four houses from each other--and said, "Brother Jim, this is it! I can't take it anymore. I just can't. This is it! Friends are gone, members are gone, deacons are mad, preacher boys have left--now the building blown down. This is it."

That was Friday night. Saturday morning I went down to the churchhouse, and folks came by the church. One thing about our church in Garland--you don't have to know what's going to happen; something is always happening. If it's not a tornado, somebody has dropped dead in the church (it has happened right in our church). Folks were driving by to look at the building.

I was crying. I said to the associate pastor, "Now, Brother Jim, this is it. You better look for a place to go because I'm quitting. I'm just going to quit!"

The next morning I got up in the pulpit. What did I preach on? On Job; what else was there to preach on? I told the people about Job, and really, honestly, I was sitting in ashes and burning and scraping my old sores and feeling sorry for myself. I got down to where I was trying to show them that God gave Job the victory and he said, "I know that my redeemer liveth." Usually I would say, "Boy, I KNOW that my Redeemer liveth," but that morning I didn't know. So I said, "I know...that my Redeemer liveth." The people didn't know either. I was going to show them where God came down and gave Job the victory, gave him children, and gave him more than he had had before, and God blessed him bountifully. I got down to that place and I said, "Look here!" I wasn't convinced myself. I said, "God is going to bless us--I know He is." I didn't know it, but I said it. "I know God is going to bless us. Look here," and I read the Scripture...and you know what it said? It said when the Lord came down to tell Job that victory had come, He came <u>in a whirlwind</u>! "Oh," I said, "Victory has come! The Lord came in a tornado and told us that victory is here, and defeat is over!"

Boy, the people shouted for joy, the choir rejoiced, and folks were saying, "Praise the Lord!" All of a sudden like a bolt out of the blue, we had a glimpse again of Him who is invisible, and from that day till this we haven't been the same.

More than anything else in the world, we need some hard times! We need some times to be broke and lonely and forsaken and forgotten! We need some enemies, some heartaches, some battles!

In my own crooked, wicked, vile life, if I didn't have heartaches and times of despondency and loneliness, I wouldn't seek help from Him. But I want you to know, when those times come and it seems like nobody understands and really you can say nobody <u>does</u> understand--nobody understands but Jesus. He is the only one who ever had the problems that we have, like we're having them.

Dr. Rice, bless his heart, will come to the rescue of anybody who stands for God anywhere--I don't care who he is. If I had my life to live over and could be born with any daddy in the world, I'd say, "Let me be John Rice's son." Walt, I congratulate you. If I had found one of these Rice girls before I married, I believe I would have been a bigamist! I really do, I really do, because I'd like to be in his family. Anyhow I appreciate him and he comes to your rescue. But even John Rice doesn't completely understand <u>your</u> problems and I don't completely understand <u>his</u> problems. Neither my little old mother nor my wife completely understand <u>my</u> problems. There are times when nobody understands, and the only hope you've got is to see Him who is invisible.

God is so good and so wonderful, and about the time we get down to the bottom of the barrel, it seems as if He lifts the shutter of Heaven and says, "Say, look at Me again." We get to see Him again and we say, "Fill 'er up. We're on our way again," and off we go. So times of heartache seem to accompany times of seeing Him who is invisible.

In the second place, it seems men who have seen Him who is invisible are lonely men. I didn't intend to say this, but I will: Don't ever get to the place where you depend upon these conferences for your spiritual strength. Get a straight line through to Heaven. Get through when there are no conferences going on! He who is invisible is available for conferences any time. Depend on fellowship with Him, speak with Him--the God who lives, the God who rained fire on Elijah, the God who filled the oil in the little lady's pots, the God who changed water to wine, the God who fed the five thousand, the God who raised His Son from the dead. He is a God who lives and you can have fellowship with Him who is invisible.

I think how lonely Dr. Rice must get. I'll tell you, loneliness is the hardest thing I've had to face since I've been preaching. I was raised in a Southern Baptist church--licensed, married, baptized, spanked, everything else in a Southern Baptist church! That's all I knew. When I started preaching my preacher preached pretty good and I thought every preacher stood against sin. So I took off with a pitchfork in one hand, to stick folks in the seat of the breeches and wake them up, and a Bible in the other, to tell them what to do when they woke up. I found out right away that everybody wasn't for me. I was brutally shocked! The pastor of the First Baptist Church where I was pastoring then didn't feel led to co-operate with me. Talk about co-operating with modernists--he wouldn't co-operate with me at all! It just seemed nobody understood.

It seems the lonelier the road has gotten, the sweeter it has been. I couldn't say that before I read about the whirlwind, but the lonelier the road has gotten, the sweeter it's been. It seems when you get to the place where you say, "Who can I turn to?" Somebody says, "Did you ever think about Me?" You look up and He pulls back the shutter and you get a glimpse of Him who is invisible.

Bearing Christ's Reproach Must Come With Seeing Him Who Is Invisible

The third thing notice very quickly. The main thing I want to say is to see Him who is invisible, you have to bear reproach. This modern-day popular Christianity is not the kind the Bible talks about--this Jane Russell type, this Roy Rogers type--teach them how to kill on Saturday and tell them what the Lord means to you on Sunday, I don't care how good the testimony is.

In Dallas they had Pat Boone down (can you feature it?) for a religious rally, packed the city auditorium with 10,000 people. Pat Boone got up there and told them what Jesus meant to him. Isn't that something? That may sound good, and Grandma, Agnes, and Oswald, you can sit out there and cry and say, "It sure is good to see a young man that is popular be so religious." I tell you what, that isn't the kind the Bible has anything to say about.

Show me anybody in the Bible worth his weight in salt who wasn't hated by the crowd. There wasn't one socially popular character in all the Bible! Abel was killed by his brother. Noah was hated by his people and could get but seven converts in preaching 120 years. Joseph was sold into slavery. Moses was hated by his family and his race. Elijah was chased until he thought he was the only one. Elisha was hated and called "bald head." The more hair I lose, the more I appreciate Elisha. He was the first bald-headed Baptist preacher boy! Isaiah preached to deaf ears. Jeremiah was a weeping prophet. Daniel was put in the lions' den. The Hebrew children were put in the fiery furnace. David was chased by Saul. John the Baptist lost his head. Peter was crucified upside down. Stephen was stoned outside the gates. Paul was left for dead outside Lystra. John was exiled on Patmos. James was martyred. Jesus Christ was put to Calvary!

How in the name of common sense do you think you can walk the streets of this world, in your city, in your town, and have folks think you are a nice fellow? You can't be a master mason, president of the Lions Club, pray at every dog show that comes into town and be the kind of preacher you ought to be. We need some John the Baptists again who will rise up in our town and call folks to repent. When you walk down the streets in your city, folks ought to spit at you, make fun of you, laugh at you. I don't mean because you want them to spit at you, but because you hold forth the banner of Calvary, the blood, the Book, the blessed hope, and fight sin, exalt Jesus Christ, and fight the things you ought to fight. I don't care where you live--they will hate you. The Bible says, "The servant is not greater than his Lord" (John 13:16). They hated Jesus and nailed Him to Calvary; they spat upon Him and plucked out His beard. Are you better than He is?

I tell my people that I want it to be so in my town that when folks drive by my church they get rebuked by looking at the building. One lady told me, "We have to drive by your church to go to work every morning, but we drive around the block to miss it." I asked, "Why?" Her reply, "We don't even want to be reminded of you."

When I walk down the street in my town and people look at me, I want them to think about the sin they are committing or have committed. I want their sin rebuked by my very presence. I often say, "When you come to Garland and mention Jack Hyles, you duck or pucker--one or the other!" You'll get hit in the mouth or kissed, I'll guarantee you for sure.

We've got the idea nowadays that a preacher is like a lawyer. The most respected folks in town--the doctor, the lawyer, and the preacher. That's the Devil's lie. There was a day when preachers ran for their lives, yet we say we're premillennialists and we say the world is getting worse. If the world is getting worse, why aren't we running for our lives? It seems to me that our churches ought to fight sin and stand against modernism and sin and unrighteousness until folks will think we are screwballs, fanatics, cranks, and fools for Christ. Yet those of us who are fundamentalists nowadays have gotten so soft. Talk about "yesterday's fundamentalists" and "second generation fundamentalists." The last generation of fundamentalists started churches in garages and tents and brush arbors and fought the city council and fought the school board. They fought for all they got. They were hated and misunderstood and laughed at. Now we have doctors' degrees and we are Rev. Hyles and Dr. Rice, Dr. Malone.

We've got Doctor of Divinity and Doctor This and Rev. This and Brother This! Our preachers have gotten so respectable we can walk down the streets in our city and folks look at us and say, "There goes a good man." The bootleggers in my town ought not to like me. The modernists ought not to like me! Some of you preachers say, "I appreciate Dr. Rice. He's gotten his name ruined in many places because of his stand." Pray tell me, why don't you go to your own little town of 500 or 1,000 and take the same stand --have the same reputation locally he has nationally? The Bible says, "Woe be unto you when all men speak well of you" (Luke 6:26), and "If I pleased men I should not be the servant of God" (Gal. 1:10). We're afraid somebody will think we're different or won't like us and we won't be respected in our town.

You say, "Brother Hyles, I don't believe in sticking your tongue out at everybody." I don't either--just at some. I'll tell you one thing: we dead sure need more fighting going on in our churches. A man yesterday said, "How do you get folks to come to your church?" I said, "I just stay in a scrap all the time. Anybody will come to watch a good fight."

A man said not long ago, "Jack, how do you get a crowd to come to hear you?" I said, "Just get against a bunch of stuff and preach against it. That's the way to do it." Like

I said last year, if you can't be against anything else, preach against Hershey bars! I mean just get a series of sermons on Hershey bars and get up there and act like you mean it. Don't get up there and say, "The trouble with our country is too many Hershey bars." Boy, get up there and say, "BROTHER, THE THING THAT IS WRONG WITH OUR COUNTRY IS THAT OUR TEETH ARE ROTTING OUT BECAUSE OF THE SUGAR IN HERSHEY BARS, AND WE NEED MORE FOLKS WHO WILL FIGHT HERSHEY BARS!" I'll guarantee you one thing--your house will be filled! You preach to empty pews and empty houses because you don't stand for anything or against anything. You are like the old Negro who said, "I jes' throws myself in neutral and whichever way you pushes I goes." That is not what God called us to do.

When I think about men of God, prophets of God of yesterday, and I think about Jeremiah who sat in the dust and cried, "Is it nothing to you, all ye that pass by? behold, and see if there be any sorrow like unto my sorrow..." (Lam. 1:12); when I think about Isaiah and how folks stopped their ears and wouldn't hear him; when I think about the head of old John the Baptist lying on the platter of the king; when I think about old Paul lying outside Lystra, I want to say, "O God, I'm sorry I'm such a sissy. I'm sorry! The same world is alive, the same Devil is alive today, and I'm sorry I don't suffer more."

Brother, if you ever want the curtain pulled back so you can see Him who is invisible, come to the place in your life where you bear His reproach.

Bible Christians Who Saw Him Who Is Invisible

Would you take a walk with me for awhile...down a little road. We see some people. As I walk down the road I wonder what I'll do for Jesus. A man beside the road is preaching. He has the Bible open, the book of the law. There are not many there--oh, some--but some stop, then pass on by. The man knows what he is talking about; he speaks with authority. I believe if that young man were a lawyer, he could be a success. If that young man were a doctor, he could be very prominent in the city. If he were a businessman, I think he could make a million, because there is something about him that looks like he has talent. He is a little crude in his tactics, yet beneath that crudeness and that uncouth attitude I see something that has possibilities.

I say, "Sir, what is your name?"

"My name is Isaiah."

"Isaiah, what are you doing?"

"I'm preaching to the people."

"Well, Isaiah, you're doing a very fine job. I don't agree with what you're saying, but listen boy, you could amount to something somewhere. If you'll just trim your message a little, the Sanhedrin would have you on the top shelf. I bet they would do you right. They'll take responsibility for you. Isaiah, look! Those folks are stopping their ears; they are hissing at you. Don't you realize you're not appreciated? Why, if you put it to a vote, they would probably vote you out next Sunday morning. You are not appreciated."

Isaiah looks at me and says, "But, sir, I'm not trying to be appreciated."

"Well, Isaiah, you are an unusual man. You're not normal."

"No sir, I'm not!"

"Well, what's the matter."

"I'll tell you. Back yonder when King Uzziah died, I saw the Lord high and holy, lifted up, and I said, 'Woe is me,' but the angel, the seraphim came and with the tongs of the altar he took a live coal and put it on my mouth and I could not help but preach. I couldn't be a doctor, I couldn't be a lawyer, I couldn't be a businessman, because you see the fire of God is upon my lips and I have seen Him who is invisible."

I scratch my head and walk on down the street. I come to another little fellow who is preaching. Pretty soon I see the crowd rise up and take stones and throw at him. He runs and pretty soon he falls beneath the stones. He is about to die. I pick him up and hold his bloody head in my hands and say, "Sir, what is your name?"

"Sir, my name is Stephen."

"You know, you ought not to be smiling now, because you're dying."

"But," he says, "Sir, you don't understand."

"Stephen, what are you?"

"Well, I'm a deacon, sir."

"A deacon? I saw you preaching."

"Yes, I'm a preaching deacon."

"I'll tell you, Stephen, it seems to me you ought to be on the finance committee where deacons ought to be. I mean you ought to be in those committee meetings trying to tell the preacher how to run the church. After all, that's what deacons are for."

"But you see, sir, God didn't call me because I was a good businessman. He didn't call me because I was smart. God called me because I was full of the Holy Ghost."

"But Stephen, old boy, you're losing your mind."

"I'm beginning to see Him who is invisible."

"Well, you're about to go off now, old boy; you're just about to crack up."

He says, "Wait a minute. I see the glory of God."

"Well, wait a minute now, don't get beside yourself."

"Oh," he said, "I see the glory of God. I see Jesus standing at the right hand of God."

"But, Stephen, I belong to the Sanhedrin and I happen to know that Jesus is not <u>standing</u> at the right hand of God; He's <u>sitting</u> there."

"Yes, but He's standing up to welcome me. I'm about to go see Him. Oh, I'm so glad I did what I did because I have seen Him who is invisible!"

I walk down the street a little ways and I come to a man, blind, groping in the dark, on the road to Damascus. I recognize him immediately to be a successful young man, one who could have reached the top in the religious field. I say, "Sir, what is the matter with you?"

"I can't see. I can see, but I can't see. I can't see you, but I sure can see lots of other things."

"Sir, you are a pretty smart fellow. I know you. I've heard you speak before. You've got talent. Listen, we'll go down and see the optometrist and he'll fix your eyes up. I'll tell you what I'll do. I'll recommend you to the First Jewish Synagogue and you will be the leading moderator of the Jewish Association. I'll see to it that you go all the way to the top."

A fellow told me that one time. He said, "Brother Jack, if you'll trim your message, you'll go all the way to the top."

I said, "I've fished some, and I know one thing. When fish are alive, they stay at the bottom; when they are dead, they come to the top. I'll stay alive!"

So I say, "But, Paul, don't you realize I'll take you to the top?"

And old Saul of Tarsus looks up and says, "Sir, I cannot." I like what he said there. He said on the road to Damascus, "Who art thou, Lord?" He didn't know who He was, but he knew whoever He was He was his Lord from then on. He said, "If you can make me feel this way, you're my Lord from now on." He said, "Who art thou, Lord? I don't know who you are but you're my Lord."

Paul says, "I've seen Him who is invisible."

I come down the road a little further and I see that same little fellow outside a city. He lies there; it seems he is unconscious. I reach for his heartbeat and there is no beat, no pulse. I say, "It's that same little fool that sold himself down the river. I knew he ought to have taken my proposition and gone to the top. I knew he should have." I reach down and I try to pick up his body and call the undertaker. I say, "Paul, Paul," but there's no answer. Pretty soon I see an eyelid flutter. I say, "Now wait a minute, be still."

But Paul looks up and he says, "Boy, this is great."

"Now wait a minute, Paul. Just be calm. We'll get the doctor in a minute. We'll make you live."

"But I don't want to live. Let me die."

"Wait a minute, Paul. You're crazy. I knew you were crazy when you gave up your job with the Baptist headquarters as the executive secretary's office boy. I knew when you did that you were dead sure crazy. But listen, Paul, you just sit there."

Paul says, "Don't worry about me." Paul gets up, brushes the blood and the dust, and all the grit and grime off, and says, "Listen, you know what I saw? You wouldn't believe it if I told you. But I saw...aw, I can't tell you. It isn't lawful for me to tell you and if I told you, you would call me a liar. But I'll tell you one thing--I've seen Him who is invisible!"

I walk down the street a little while longer. I come to three young men inside a furnace. I say, "Young man, what's your name?"

"My name is Shadrach."

"Sir, what's yours?"

"Meshach."

"What's yours?"

"Abed-nego."

I say, "I've seen you fellows before. You were training to be leaders in the kingdom during the captivity period, weren't you?"

"Yes, sir."

"And here you are. What are you doing in the fiery furnace?"

Shadrach says, "Shoot, boy, who turned the air-conditioning on?"

Meshach says, "Ooooch, it's cold; I need my overcoat."

But I say, "Wait a minute, fellows. You're just about to

die now. What's wrong with you? What are you in there for?"

"Well, the king built up an old image out here and said bow down and worship it. We could have done it. The king said if we didn't do it we would get thrown in the fiery furnace."

Just about that time I see a fellow coming. It is the king! Standing at attention, I say, "Hello, your majesty." (I'm trying to get to the top, you know.) "Hello, your majesty," and I salute.

The king says, "Wait a minute. Those three men are supposed to be dead. Why, they have been in that furnace long enough to have burned to a...oh!...Who put the extra one in there?"

Old Shadrach looks up and says, "Sir, the extra one is He who is invisible."

I go on down the street and see a young man praying at a window. I ask, "Young man, what are you doing?"

"I'm praying."

"What's your name?"

"Daniel."

"Well, Daniel, you know it's not right to pray, don't you?"

"Yes."

"Don't you realize that you're next in command? You'll go to the top of the kingdom. If you will just quit praying in front of that window you can get to the top of the kingdom and witness to everybody in Congress and win the whole Congress to the Lord. Daniel, if you'll just keep your mouth shut for awhile right here, someday you can be at the top and you might win the whole empire and win the world and bring in the kingdom. You might do it."

Daniel says, "No, I've got to pray. If I don't pray here, I'll deny my God. I've got to pray."

"But don't you realize, young man, you've got a future ahead of you? Stop and think! Don't run with that John Rice crowd. He'll ruin your reputation. Your reputation is gone if you appear on the same program with Jack Hyles and Tom Malone and John Rice and these others. Now wake up! Get some sense into your head, you little crazy nincompoop! Get some sense in your head."

Daniel says, "Sir, I cannot do it, because I have seen Him who is invisible."

I walk down the road a little further and see an old gray-haired man who hasn't had a haircut in years. His beard comes down across his chest and his locks flow down over his shoulders. He has one of the sweetest looks on his face you have ever seen. I say to him, "Sir, what is your name?"

"My name is John."

"John, how many folks live on this island here?"

"One."

"I see that old age is affecting you some. What is the population?"

"One."

"I guess you are that one."

"Yes."

"Well, I want you to know, old man, I love you and I appreciate you. You have my sympathy."

"Why sympathy, sir?"

"Well, I know it must get awful lonely out here."

"Lonely? Oh, no, for I've seen seraphims and angels and cherubim. I've seen the great wedding feast and the marriage of the Lamb. I've seen the saints coming in the clouds of glory and all of them on white horses. I've seen the millennium. I've even seen the golden streets of the new Jerusalem."

I say, "Now, fellow, sometimes when one gets up in years he has hallucinations like that."

"Oh," he said, "don't worry about me, because all these years out here I have been seeing Him who is invisible."

I don't know about you, but I'm tired of deadness and

coldness. I'm tired of formality. I'm tired of going to church and just studying and going home. I want to see Him who is invisible, don't you? Don't you want again somehow a breath of God, and to hear from Heaven and pull the curtain back and once again see Him who is invisible?

I see a little fellow leading a band of Israelites. I hear one of them cry, "Oh, you rascal. We wish we were back eating cucumbers and leeks and garlic in Egypt, and you led us out here." The other one says, "Yeah, I make a motion your work is finished here. I feel some man who can work with young people might be better qualified for the position. Yeah, I make a move we do."

God says, "Moses, what shall I do?"

Moses said, "Kill them."

"No," God says.

Pretty soon God said, "Okay, I'm ready to kill them."

Moses said, "No, God, don't do it after all."

Somebody said if Moses and God had ever gotten in the killing mood at the same time, there wouldn't have been anybody left but God and Moses!

Moses said, "No, no, don't kill them."

I walk up and I say, "Moses, aren't you the young man I used to see over there in the Egyptian palace?"

"Yes, sir, I am."

"Well, Moses, it's nice to have a hobby, some recreation, but I'm sure you are the head of the great kingdom now."

"No, sir, they won't let me in the palace anymore."

"Well, what did you do?"

"I went and tried to get freedom for the Israelites."

"Israelites! You did?"

"Yes, you know back yonder when I was in the wilderness, I was keeping some sheep one day and I looked over and saw a bush burning down--it just kept burning down. I walked down the road a little piece and looked back and that bush was still burning. I looked up there, and you know, I saw Him who is invisible in that bush. He said, 'I want you to do my work.' I said, 'I can't do it, I haven't got anything.' "

Listen! Did you know God does better work with folks who haven't got anything when He calls them, than He does with folks that have a bunch of stuff. That's why I'd rather get converts from folks a little ignorant; they haven't got to unlearn a bunch of stuff. You just start with nothing.

Moses said, "I haven't got anything."

God said, "What have you got in your hand?"

Moses said, "I've got a rod."

"Throw it on the ground!"

It became a snake.

God said, "Pick it up." (I don't know about you, but that's where me and Moses would have parted company right there.) Now I want you to get this. I'm no theologian but I can read in the Bible and I get some thoughts once in awhile. If Moses had not thrown that whole rod on the ground, Moses would have had half of that snake in his hand. I don't know theology, but that's true, and I believe he would have had the biting half! Boy, the most dangerous thing you'll ever do is to give God half your life. Give Him all of it!

I say, "But Moses, what is the matter with you? Why, don't you realize you could be the leader of a kingdom?"

But Moses says, "No, I could not be disobedient to the heavenly vision, because I have seen Him who is invisible."

As I look at the hall of heroes, I bow in shame and say, "O God, I'm a sissy! There's Moses--he gave up a kingdom; there's Paul--he gave up a future; there's John--he lost his head; and Abraham--he lost his home; and the Lord Jesus--He lost everything on earth."

And I sing with the poet,

Must I be carried to the skies
On flow'ry beds of ease,
While others fought to win the prize,
And sailed thro' bloody seas?

Sure I must fight, if I would reign,
Increase my courage, Lord;
I'll bear the toil, endure the pain,
Supported by Thy word.

if every once in awhile You'll just pull the curtain and let me see Him who is invisible.

5

How to Fire the Preacher

"Then flew one of the seraphims unto me, having a live coal in his hand, which he had taken with tongs from off the altar: And he laid it upon my mouth, and said, Lo, this hath touched thy lips; and thine iniquity is taken away, and thy sin purged. Also I heard the voice of the Lord, saying, Whom shall I send, and who will go for us? Then said I, Here am I; send me."--Isa. 6:6-8.

"And when the day of Pentecost was fully come, they were all with one accord in one place. And suddenly there came a sound from heaven as of a rushing mighty wind, and it filled all the house where they were sitting. And there appeared unto them cloven tongues like as of fire, and it sat upon each of them."--Acts 2:1-3.

I love preachers. In the front of my Bible I keep a list of the number of preachers who hear me in every service across the country. Every time I preach, I write down the number of preachers in the audience. In the United States and Canada, I thank God that I have been able to speak to 4,095 different preachers as far as I know, this year.

I always want to preach to preachers. I love preachers. No one in America needs loving like the preacher does. Let me say this: The greatest thing in this world is to preach the Gospel of Jesus Christ. I'm not asking for your sympathy, but for your fellowship and your loyalty.

There are some preachers in this service whose hearts

are broken. In this conference one preacher said to me, "Pray for me."

I said, "What do you mean?"

He said, "I won't be there long unless a miracle takes place."

I said, "How does it stack up?"

He said, "Two to one against me."

I asked, "Why?"

He said, "I have been preaching against sin and trying to clean up the church and get folks to walk right."

I know preacher after preacher in this area who has decided to stand for God, but whose heart has been broken and who is tottering tonight on his job. One of these days Jack Hyles and some others who have preached here will step aside for some of you fellows who have had smaller crowds but who have dared to stand true; who have lost your job, and lost your church because you have dared stand for God. I love the men of God.

A few years ago I was in Winston-Salem in one of these conferences. Dr. Rice was preaching and I was sitting on the front row. Bud Lyles was leading the singing. Bud asked the preachers to sit in the choir. About 45 preachers came. Now I haven't a bit of use for a pussy-footing, back-scratching, ear-tickling, rose-water, pink tea-and-lemonade preacher. But I love the men of God who stand for the Bible. There's nothing I would rather do than be a blessing to preachers. I wish the Lord tonight would let me skin some of you old preacher-killers so you would ask God to forgive your sins and keep that Hell-fire-and-brimstone preacher behind your pulpit. I wish God would save some preacher tonight from a wicked and untoward congregation, and if need be, save a church tonight.

When I looked at those preachers in the choir, I said, "God bless them." Out of about 45 preachers there, there wasn't enough hair on all the heads to cover one good-sized head! Isn't it amazing what God can do with a little lump of clay. Seven out of 45 had on green ties with navy blue suits! Praise the Lord for them. God bless the preachers!

You don't know how much the preacher needs the help of the lay people. Let me say this too: The problems in this country could be solved with preaching. There is not a problem we have--from the juvenile delinquency problem all the way up and down--that couldn't be solved with a generation of preachers. The only vocation in the world that has a large segment of our people listening to them every week is the ministry. There is nothing in the world this country needs more than a generation of Elijahs and Isaiahs to preach the truth to our people.

"But," you say, "they won't like it."

Who in the world ever said they were supposed to like it?

In this same Winston-Salem conference we were having testimonies one afternoon. One lady jumped up and said, crying, "I want to thank God. I guess I am the only lady here who was saved under her own preaching." Dr. Rice looked up rather startled, and all of us were waiting to see what would happen. She said, "I used to play church when I was a little girl. One would lead singing, one would preach, and one would give the invitation. The next day we would change and do something different. One morning it was my time to preach. The only kind of preaching I had ever heard was Hell-fire-and-brimstone preaching. I was a little six-year-old girl and I preached, 'All of you younguns had better get born again or you're going to burn in Hell.' "

She said, "All of a sudden it dawned on me I had not been born again. I stopped the preaching, went back to the back of the room, came down the aisle, and got converted under my own preaching!"

God deliver me from these teacher-type preachers. Now I believe you ought to teach. But brother, preaching is teaching with a tear in its eye. If we don't have some preaching again in the Chicago area, we are gone. Listen, if the deeper life conferences would save America, we would be in the millennium right now! All some of you folks do is get the Bible and study it like a math book while the world goes to Hell. If we don't get some old Hell-fire-and-brimstone, Hell-raising, sin-fighting, Christ-honoring, soul-winning, evangelistic, Bible preaching in Chicago, WE'RE GONE! I like what the old Pentecostal preacher said down South. Instead of saying, "God called me to heal the sick, and raise the dead, and cast out devils," he got his tange all toungled up and it came out, "God has called me to heal the dead, cast out the sick, and raise the Devil." That's what we need in Chicago.

If some of you preachers would raise more devil on Sunday morning, your deacons would raise less devil on Saturday night. We need some Elijahs who have been with God, and who will pray down fire from Heaven, who are on fire. We need some John Wesleys who will say, "I just set myself on fire and folks come to watch me while I burn."

We need some Isaiahs whose lips have been touched with the coals from off the altar, and they are on fire for God. We need some Emmaus apostles who said, "Our hearts did burn within us while we walked with Him." We need some preachers and we need some pulpits on fire with the Gospel of the Lord Jesus Christ.

"But," you say, "I'm not a preacher. What can I do?"

You have no idea how much you could do. How many times have you preachers gone to your study, gotten on your face (nobody knows how much a preacher who loves the Bible pours his soul out alone) and said, "O God, do something for me. Do something for me. Do something for the people." Then you come on Sunday morning and the crowd is dead, or folks stayed home, or they are on the lake fishing or some went home after Sunday school. Some are hoping you will get through right quick, and some are sound asleep. I'm just saying, you don't know what you can do for a preacher dear friends. YOU CAN FIRE YOUR PREACHER. If you would <u>fire</u> him, you wouldn't have to <u>fire</u> him.

If you would set him on fire, if you would spend as much time praying for him as you do criticizing him and use the same amount of words, you would be surprised what it might do for him.

People help make a preacher. Dr. Herschel Ford said that preaching is simply pouring back in a flood what you get from the people in a vapor. Many a preacher started out in his twenties to preach the truth, but broke on the anvil of some old hard-headed, bull-headed deacon who wanted to see how many preachers he could ruin. As I look back at my ministry, a great deal of what little success I have enjoyed I owe to those godly people who down through these almost seventeen years have stuck by this little preacher.

I recall dear Sister Waldrop who used to sit over on the right, who sang so beautifully. She was almost four times my age. She used to call me and say, "Pastor, I need some advice." I used to think she really needed it, but now realize she just wanted to make me feel I was her pastor. I thank God for those people.

I. ONE ACCORD

You ask, "Preacher, what can I do?" First, you can be in one accord in one place doing one thing. One accord--that will fire your preacher. In one place--that will fire your preacher. All doing the same thing--that will fire your preacher. We ought to be in one accord behind the preacher.

Now if you have one of these little preachers who doesn't believe the Bible is the inspired Word of God, if he says this Bible is not inspired literally, every jot, every tittle, every word in the original inspired of God; if he says it is only thought inspired, FIRE HIM! If you can't fire him, get out. Some folks say, "But Granddaddy is buried in the cemetery behind the church." Well, dig him up and take him over to another cemetery. I am sick in my soul of people dying in a cold, liberal, dead church because a tombstone is in the back yard. If you can't fire the liberal, then get out of his church and go where somebody can preach the Word of God to your family.

I have some statistics about preachers, put out by Mr. Gallup. How accurate they are, I cannot say. He said, "In America, in our country, only five per cent of our ministerial students believe the creation story of Genesis. Only 24 per cent believe the miracles of the Bible. Only 26 per cent believe the Bible is the Word of God. Only 25 per cent believe in the virgin birth." This is Gallup talking.

"Only 11 per cent of our young preachers believe in Hell. Only 11 per cent of our young preachers believe in Heaven. Only 18 per cent of our young preachers believe in the literal resurrection of Christ. Only 13 per cent of our young preachers believe in the depravity of man. Only 21 per cent of our young preachers believe that God hears and answers prayer."

With an area and a country and a world infested with men who do not believe this Book, let me say this: If you have a man behind your pulpit who believes in the Bible, who preaches the truth, who fights the Devil, who is not scared of a member he has in his church, who will preach what God says preach, in God's dear name, forget how he combs his hair and back him up! (Many preachers' hearts are broken because they don't have a wave in their hair.) Why could Peter stand up on Pentecost and preach in power? Because the people were in one accord. Stay behind your pastor in his preaching.

Moses' hands were heavy in the battle with the Amalekites, and Aaron and Hur were on his side. They lifted up his hands and the battle was won. When they let down his hands, the battle was lost (Exod. 17:10-13). If you have a preacher who preaches the truth of God every time he gets in the pulpit, when he walks out in the pulpit, you say, "Dear Lord, thank you that in my pulpit, preaching to my children, is a man who believes the Bible is the Word of

God and fights sin and exalts Christ and wins souls to Christ." Stand behind him.

When I first started preaching down in East Texas, the chairman of my deacons was L. G. Eaves, Sr. When I stood up that night to preach my trial sermon in that little country church, I looked out and saw a man who had one leg and a sawed-off crutch (I didn't know then he was chairman of the deacons). He would put that leg out ready to put it down when the preacher said something good. The first time I said something good, which was about 30 minutes after I started back in those days, he put that old foot down and shouted "AMEN." That shook me up. I almost did not get back on my subject. Revival broke out in that little country church. We only had seven prospects, but 27 consecutive Sundays folks were saved. One Sunday we had people saved and joined the church who lived 80 miles from each other. One lived 40 miles down this way on a little country road; the others lived 40 miles up this way. The people used to say, "Let's go hear that little preacher out there, that little loud-mouth fellow."

But one of the main reasons under God there was success and revival was because God gave some faithful country people who would walk with God and stand behind the preacher.

When I was in Texas preaching, J. B. Combest preached more than I did. He almost preached me to death. If he was hot, he would say more words in a sermon than I did! I would preach; he would say, "That's right. Amen! Oh, that's what it says in the Book. Oh, preacher, let 'em have it! Hey, pull over and park there for a little while." J. Harold Smith was preaching one night in our church, and he said, "I'm like Jeremiah. Sometimes I get so full, I just can't contain myself. I just get so full sometimes, I can't hold it in."

Old J. B. said, "Then, preacher, LET IT OUT!"

Ah, those people were behind the preacher. Some of you

fellows holler like Comanche Indians at a football game but sit like wooden Indians on Sunday morning. We need once again some people on Sunday morning who, when the preacher walks in the pulpit, will realize that God's man is coming into God's place, and who will sit expectantly and prayerfully while he preaches and give him a good old loud AMEN once in a while. I hope I'll wake up some of you deadhead deacons in these churches around here and teach you how to say amen. You say, "It just ruffles my nerves." It's not that that ruffles your nerves, but that old Hell-fire-and-brimstone preaching that ruffles your nerves.

One little fellow said to me when I first came to Hammond, "My wife cannot come to hear you preach. Your hollering disturbs her."

I said, "It's not my hollering; it's what I holler that disturbs her."

Listen, if all you want is a sedate, high church service on Sunday morning, get the obituary column and become a traveling funeral director. You won't find a thing in the book of Acts about your so-called high church service on Sunday morning.

Back up your pastor in his preaching. Say "Amen" every once in a while. If you want a preacher who really cuts loose and preaches, then help him along occasionally.

A fellow told me about a church in Arkansas that had a sermon committee. I said, "What kind of a committee is that?"

"Well, they have a committee of three people that checks on the preacher's sermon. The preacher gets the sermon up all week, gives it to the sermon committee on Saturday. The sermon committee reads it and approves it or rejects it, then gives it back to him." He said, "Boy, that's terrible, isn't it?"

I said, "I have the same thing."

"Oh, not you! Not you!"

I said, "Yes, me."

He said, "A sermon committee?"

I said, "A sermon committee."

He said, "That tells you what to preach?"

I said, "One that checks on my sermons."

He said, "How many are on it?"

I said, "Three--GOD THE FATHER, GOD THE SON, AND GOD THE HOLY GHOST."

One of my deacons said to me once, "Brother Hyles, about your sermon Sunday morning...."

I said, "Hold on there! When we paint the ceiling, you get one vote. When we put new pews in, you get one vote. When we build a building, you get one vote. But when I preach, you don't get no votes."

I have told my deacons many a time, "From here to here and all the way over to here (the pulpit), IS MINE. Leave it alone." Oh, wouldn't it be wonderful if God once again would raise up some prophets and some people who would follow them.

Can you feature those old settlers, Charles G. Finney, Jonathan Edwards, Dwight Moody and Billy Sunday, kow-towing to a bunch of worldly folks? Sam Jones said, "When I first started preaching, I used to be afraid I would make somebody mad. Now I'm afraid I won't."

Back him up in his preaching. Somebody is always saying to me, "Brother Hyles, I like to have an evangelist come to my church so he can say some things that the pastor can't say." I would resign and quit preaching if I were you. Brother, there's not an evangelist in America who can say anything in the First Baptist Church of Hammond that I can't say. And if I couldn't say it, I'd quit. I think prophets ought to be prophets, and preachers ought to be preachers. And listen, your folks would love you for it. One good thing about old Hell-fire-and-brimstone preaching is that the folks who are right with God love it, and the folks who are not right with God need it, so let them have it! PREACH!

You people stand behind the preacher. And you deacons leave him alone.

I promised God on my knees when I started preaching, "I'm not a great preacher, but one thing I won't do, dear Lord, and that is to let anybody tell me what to preach."

If God would give us people who would go to the preacher before he preaches and say, "We really need it this morning; let us have it; preach the Word," it would set some preachers loose.

Let me say this. Pray for him. You will fire him by praying for him. The loneliest person in your church is your pastor. The only person in the church who cannot pick up the phone and call some friend and ask them over for dinner is the pastor. The only person in your church who has no one to call when he goes to the hospital or is seriously ill is the pastor. The only person in your church who has no pastor is your pastor.

One of the saddest things in my life, and yet one of the sweetest things, was the day when it dawned upon me on my knees in a pine thicket in East Texas that I had no pastor and would never have a pastor. My little wife and I got on our knees beside a ditch under a pine tree in East Texas and opened our Bible and we said, "Dear Lord, we don't have a pastor. We're going to have to depend upon You."

I am not asking for sympathy, but for loyalty and fellowship on the part of you who follow us preachers. Pray for us. You don't know where we are. You wake up at night some night and toss and turn at 2 o'clock in the morning. Your pastor might be at the hospital leaning over trying to tell some poor dying lost man how to be saved. Your pastor might be at the funeral home trying to console some family. He might be traveling through the air somewhere at night trying to get to the next preaching appointment the next morning so he can help somebody else to get on fire for God. Pray for your pastor.

At 2 o'clock in the morning in Garland, Texas, I was

burdened. We were having all-night prayer in those days, and I decided to go down and pray at the church for awhile. We had a prayer room. When I got to the prayer room I heard someone pray, "Dear Lord, bless my preacher. I love him. Lord, I would be on my way to Hell if it were not for him. He taught me about Jesus and prayed for me and preached to me and...Lord bless the pastor." I stood outside the door about 15 minutes and listened to that dear deacon call my name in prayer. You think that didn't put some fire in my bones?

Never a little boy or girl comes up to me and sits on my knee and says, "Brother Hyles, I pray for you every night," that there isn't a thrill goes through my heart. Oh, pray for the preacher. Fire him. Pray for him. Every time the family kneels to pray, pray for God to bless the preacher. Pray for God to turn him loose, and pray for God to set him on fire. Pray for the preacher. A lot of preachers here need it desperately tonight.

I was in Windsor, Ontario, Canada, preaching at one of the largest churches in Ontario. When I finished, I went upstairs to the pastor's study. The pastor, a godly man, and I were talking about the service. Somebody knocked on the door. We waited just a second, then we continued talking. In the middle of a sentence the knock came again. All of a sudden, the door burst open and in came a big fellow about 6 foot 2. He draped himself across that preacher and said, "Preacher, I'm sorry."

And the preacher said, "Sorry about what? What's wrong?"

"I have been criticizing you. I haven't loved you. And I would be going to Hell if it weren't for you. I ought to be shot for criticizing you."

Ah, some of you can criticize everything about your preacher--the way he walks, the way he stands up. If he hollers, he hollers too loud. If he doesn't holler, he doesn't holler loud enough. Brother, if you have a bellowing foghorn like my folks have, bless God, he bellows the truth. And if you have some little quiet fellow who talks in a real quiet voice and preaches the truth and fights the Devil and hates sin and exalts the Saviour, stick with him. Set him on fire. Encourage him.

II. ONE PLACE

Not only that, but they were all in one accord, in one place. If you want to set your preacher on fire, be faithful. We have a lot of "used-to-was-ers" in our churches, "has-been-ers" and "gonna-do-ers" and "used-to-be-ers." I want some "doin'-now-ers." Be faithful.

Someone asks, "Brother Hyles, what kind of folks would you like to build your church on? Rich people?"

"No."

"Talented?"

"No."

"Well-to-do?"

"No."

"Socially acceptable?"

"No."

"Nice looking?"

"No."

"Young?"

"No."

"Old?"

"No."

"What is the one attribute that you would rather have in your members than any other single attribute?"

The answer is one word: "Faithful." If you want to set your preacher on fire, you be there.

Do you know what I'm going to do for some of you ladies some time? I'm going to ask you to invite me over to eat, and I'm going to tell you what I want. I want fried chicken, and T-bone steaks, and boiled ham, and any other meat besides those you want to fix will be okay. I want pecan pie, and banana pudding and mashed potatoes and gravy. I want you to spend seven days getting the house ready. On Monday fix the meat; on Tuesday, the dessert. I want you to work hard. Then I'm going to call you about 12:15 on Sunday and say, "I hate to tell you this but company just came in, and I haven't seen them in a long time. I know you'll understand." I want to listen to you fume on the telephone!

Well, I prepare my sermons just like you prepare a meal. I already have the diet cooked up that I am going to feed my people in the fall. When a preacher on his face seven days a week prays for God to give him power and prays for God to give him a sermon, and he very carefully and in detail prepares his sermon, and because Aunt Susie comes in, you don't show up, no wonder your preacher is not on fire for God. You be faithful.

Mamma used to say, "Son, we can't give as much as anybody, but we can be there as much as anybody." Every Sunday morning and every Sunday night since I was a little boy, I have been in church. Wife and I were married in North Carolina in the service. I was in the paratroopers. We lived a mile from the church. One night it came a gullywasher--lightning, thundering electrical storm. We didn't have a car, we didn't have an umbrella, we didn't have a raincoat, we didn't have rubber shoes or anything. I said, "Sweetheart, the dear Lord understands. We can't go to prayer meeting tonight. Look at that rain outside."

She said, "Of course we can't get out in that kind of weather to go to prayer meeting."

I had never missed before or since, since I was a boy. It's amazing when folks say, "I'll try to come," how many times they will be there if they try. I have been trying to be there for years and never missed but one time, and I didn't try then.

"Let's just stay here," my wife said, "and have a prayer meeting ourselves." So we prayed about 30 seconds and listened to the radio the rest of the evening (as you do).

You say, "I can worship God on the creek bank just as

well as I can in church." Yes, but you don't. That's why you didn't send your tithe in when you went fishing that Sunday.

Back to my story. We went to bed about 9 o'clock and slept till 10, 11, 12, 1, 2--and about 3 o'clock in the morning I thought a tornado had hit or an explosion. I went one way and the wife went the other, and the cover went still another way. My wife was over in this corner and I was over in the other corner. I looked and there she was, with a pillow on one shoulder and a quilt draped over the other. She was a sight. She had meringue on her face and hardware in her hair--a sight to behold! She looked over at me and I was in a terrible fix. The bed had broken down in the middle of the night. There I was over here and there she was over there. She looked up and said, "Let's go next Wednesday night."

I said, "I'll be there."

Brother, I haven't missed since! I believe in faithfulness to God's house and God's program. That preacher of yours deserves your faithfulness. Set him on fire.

You people don't realize the burdens a pastor has. You don't realize the times your pastor goes in a side room at the funeral home and cries his eyes out in order to get it over with so that he can go in and conduct a funeral service of some precious baby or someone he loves like his own life, with his heart broken. He wants to cry, but he can't cry. He goes and cries his eyes out and gets it over with, then walks in the pulpit with dry eyes. You don't understand that.

Some of you folks have pastors who are having a rough time. You can't know the times he cries himself to sleep at night. You don't understand it. You wait sometime until you have hundreds and hundreds of people on your shoulders. Here's one going away from God; here's one going back into the world; here's a home broken up; and all day long you do nothing, nothing, nothing, but counsel with homes that are breaking and counsel with boys and girls whose lives are ruined. You wait someday, and then some little old fellow criticizes you because of the way you drive your car down the street. You'll want to kill him. I'm saying, in God's name, if you have a man of God, support him. Pray for him. Be faithful, in one place.

III. ONE PURPOSE

I hasten to say: in one purpose. They were all in one accord, in one place, and they prayed, and the power of God filled the room where they were sitting, and cloven tongues like unto fire came upon them. Peter was sitting over here, and he said, "Man, I'd like to preach. Boy, I've been praying these ten days, and look at that crowd gathering. O boy, something is burning inside my soul."

That's the kind of preaching we need. Fellows who can't shut up! The rulers said, "Fellows, you can't speak anymore in the name of Jesus."

They said, "Well, hurry up and tell us whether we can preach or not, because we're going to preach anyhow. For we cannot but speak the things we have seen and heard."

Peter said, "I've got to preach." All of a sudden he got up and said, "Men and brethren, hearken unto my words." Boy, he was on fire! Why? Because people were there for one purpose, and that was to pray down the fire of God and get people born again. Listen, do you want to set your preacher on fire? Then get out tomorrow and win about three souls to Christ, and right before he preaches Sunday morning, you walk up and say, "Brother Pastor, may I speak a word to you before you go in the pulpit, please?"

The pastor says, "Yes, may I help you? Who's mad at me now?"

And you say, "Nobody I know, Pastor, but I've got some people sitting out there I won to Christ yesterday, and they're going to walk the aisle this morning."

After he revives, he will be a great preacher that morning. Do you want to set him on fire? You just say, "We'll live and we'll eat and we'll sleep this matter of soul winning." You go up to the pastor and say, "Pastor, pray for my folks! They're out there in the service this morning. Oh, I want you to pray that God will save them this morning. Pray that the Lord will reach them for Christ." Oh listen, one purpose, just one purpose.

I must close. I think back to that little song leader at the Morris Chapel Baptist Church. We only had one deacon and 19 members in a little old country half-time church. God bless old Deacon Wood Armstrong. On vacation a few years ago I drove back to the little church, and they were without a pastor.

I saw Wood outside beside the road, and I said, "Hey, Mr. Armstrong!" He didn't know me; I was double the size I was when I was his pastor.

He said, "Yes Sir?"

I said, "I understand you are a deacon up here at the Morris Chapel Baptist Church?"

"Yes Sir."

"I understand you are pastorless."

"Yes Sir."

"I'd like to apply."

"Well, we have a man in mind."

I said, "Forget about him. You've never heard anybody until you've heard me."

He looked at me and his eyes bugged out. "Sir, we don't believe--"

I said, "Believe, nothing. When you hear me, you'll forget every other preacher you have ever heard in your life." I said, "HIRE ME!"

He said, "Well, we haven't heard you yet."

I said, "I'll guarantee me."

He looked at me, and said, "Are you Jack Hyles?"

I said, "Yes, I'm Jack Hyles." He hugged me. But I recall those days. The wife and I would go out 100 miles from home, with no place to eat. We would walk out and shake hands with the little old crowd of 19 members as they walked out the door. A fellow would walk out and say, "Would you like to a---"

I would say, "Yes, yes, yes?"

He would say, "Would you like to pray for my family? We're having trouble."

Old Wood would be the last one out. He'd say, "Well, Brother pastor, if ye ain't got nowhere else to go, you can always eat black-eyed peas at out house."

And I'd say, "Well, a--well, now are you sure? Now--I'LL GO, I'LL GO." God used that little man to fire his preacher. How I thank God for him!

I would just like to say without elaborating that the people in our church who are hearing me preach tonight are among the most faithful, loyal people I have seen. They stood by me when they didn't know me well. By faith, they stood by this preacher. I'll be eternally grateful, for whatever success ever happens on the corner of Oakley Street and Sibley Street in Hammond, Indiana, will be because of some loyal, faithful people who stood by a man of God. I'm saying, my precious friend, if you have to die for your preacher, do it.

While in a revival campaign in Mesquite, Texas, I cut loose one night on fishing on Sunday. I didn't know the chairman of the board of deacons had taken some deacons fishing the Sunday before, and this was Monday night. I preached nearly a whole sermon about it. One of the deacons was going to whip me the next night. He said, "I'll get that little preacher if it's the last thing I do." And he could have gotten me well, too.

The next night I walked out and was scared stiff. When I walked out I didn't even look at the people. Finally I peeked --and saw the sweetest thing. Across the front were some of the deacons of the Miller Road Baptist Church in Garland, Texas. One of them came up and said, "Preacher, we heard you were in trouble. Just motion when you need us."

Man, I was mean that night! Boy, I tore them up! Why? Because the people had fired the preacher. You folks who want to call a committee to fire the preacher, you might fire the preacher right.

When I think about these things, so many folks come to my mind. Let me say this. On Saturday night about 9 o'clock pray for your preacher. When you go to church on Sunday, pray for your preacher. When he preaches, pray for your preacher.

This is not a part of this sermon, but I want to use it. When I was in Texas, God gave us one of the sweetest members I have ever seen. His name was James W. Moore. He had been preaching for fifty years up around Iowa and Illinois. He was 72 years of age when he came to our church in Texas. His health was broken. His hair was as white as the snow. Brother Jim and Dorothy will recall how we used to put a platform rocker over here on the side so Brother Moore could sit comfortably every Sunday. He had preached his voice out. All he had was a little squeaky voice. We always said down where I came from, if you weren't hoarse on Monday, you pussy-footed on Sunday. Brother Moore preached and preached, and finally he came to our town and retired. His health was gone. Every Sunday he would sit over on the left. Never will I forget the night Georgie Havens came to our church, Brother Moore almost shouted. He would clap his little hands while I preached on Sunday, and say, "Amen, amen, amen." I would preach. Oh, he would stir me. He would come out after the service and say (he knew all the great preachers by name in the last generation), "That's a good sermon there, Paul."

I'd say, "Paul? I'm Jack."

"Oh," he would say, "I thought you were Paul Rader there for awhile the way you preached this morning."

The next Sunday he would come out and say, "Amen, amen, amen. That's a good sermon there, Billy."

I would say, "Billy?"

"Aw, that's right. You're not Billy Sunday, but you just preach like him."

And I would love him and pat him on the back. Often on Monday he would walk in the office and our secretary, Mrs. Holland, would say, "Brother Hyles, Brother Moore is here to see you." About 9 o'clock every Monday morning he would walk in.

Sometimes I would say, "Tell him I'm busy."

She would say, "Brother Hyles, are you sure that's what you want me to tell him?"

I'd say, "Send him in." And that dear little old preacher, stoop-backed, long flowing white hair, would walk into my study. Here's what he would say, "Brother Jack" (never looking at me), "I just came by to tell you about a mistake I made when I was a kid preacher. Foolish mistake. Thought I'd tell you about it."

He'd tell me, and oddly enough, it was always the same mistake I had made the day before in my preaching. But he would never criticize me. He would never tell me that I had made a mistake. I would hug him and say, "I get you. I know what you mean."

He would leave. I loved him and he loved me. Never once did he criticize me. One night about midnight on Sunday, the telephone rang. I had gone to bed. A lady said, "This is the nurse at the local hospital. An old white-haired man is here. He's dying with a heart attack. All we know is that his name is Moore and he keeps crying, "Brother Jack, Brother Jack, Brother Jack."

I got up, put my suit on over my pajamas, and went down to the hospital, and down to his room. I asked the other fellows there, and the nurse, to leave. He had an oxygen mask on his face, and I could tell he was dying. I felt his arm. There was no pulse to be felt. He looked up at me, and said, "Brother Jack, I just want to tell you about a Bible Conference I want you to have. I want you to have Dr.

Roberson, Brother Roloff, and so and so and so and so. I'm going to go Home now. I'm going to see Paul and Peter, and Elijah and Isaiah. Is there anything you want me to tell them?"

I said, "Well, tell them I am on my way. I'll be there."

After we had talked awhile, as if he had planned it that way, he reached up and took the oxygen mask off his face and placed it over on one side of the bed. He reached out and took my hand in his old cold hand in death, and looked up at me just like he had made a plan to do it. In one last breath he said, "Brother Jack, Brother Jack, keep--preaching-- it---." He put his right hand over his heart, and his left hand formed a cross over his breast. He put his chin next to his breast. I heard angels' wings and the angels said, "Would you please step out. We have a job to perform." I slipped out in the hall, and heard the rustling of angels' wings as they took that great old spirit over to the other side of Jordan and put it in Jesus' hands. After they had taken the spirit across, the angels took their flight.

I went back into the room and said, "Dear Lord, help me to die like that. And help me to keep preaching. Help me to keep preaching it."

The only hope we have is that some preachers, some prophets, some men of God, will preach the truth.

An old man, traveling a lone highway,
Came at the evening cold and gray,
To a chasm deep and wide.
Through which was flowing a sullen tide.

The old man crossed in the twilight dim,
For the sullen stream held no fears for him.
But he turned when he reached the other side,
And builded a bridge to span the tide.

"Old man," cried a fellow pilgrim near,
"You are wasting your strength with building here;
Your journey will end with the ending day,
And you never again will pass this way.

"You have crossed the chasm deep and wide.
Why build you a bridge at eventide?"
And the builder raised his old gray head:
"Good friend, on the path I have come," he said,
"There followeth after me today
A youth whose feet will pass this way.

"This stream, which has been as naught to me,
To that fair-haired boy may a pitfall be;
He, too, must cross in the twilight dim--
Good friend, I am building this bridge for him."

God give us some preachers, fearless preachers, prophets of God, John the Baptists, Nathans, Elijahs, Isaiahs, Jeremiahs, Haggais! God give us some prophets who will preach. And God give us some people who will fire them while they preach.

6

Proper Attitudes Toward Our Lord's Return

> "For then must he often have suffered since the foundation of the world: but now once in the end of the world hath he appeared to put away sin by the sacrifice of himself. And as it is appointed unto men once to die, but after this the judgment: So Christ was once offered to bear the sins of many; and unto them that look for him shall he appear the second time without sin unto salvation."--Heb. 9:26-28.

Notice especially those words: "...unto them that look for him shall he appear the second time without sin unto salvation."

When I decided that God had called me to preach, I planned to go away to school. Mrs. Hyles and I were the only ones in the family then. That was four children ago! When we decided that God wanted us to go to school we had $40 and a black cat. We couldn't get a thing for the black cat! So we took off for school.

The last Sunday before going to school I was at my home church. My pastor was an elderly man, a godly man. As I was sitting in the service that Sunday he said, "Now listen to this carefully--," and so I listened carefully. He said, "You won't get this much in college," and I listened. And he told the entire picture of the second coming of the Lord Jesus Christ.

I went away to school, and I think, as far as schools go, I picked a good school. I had to study and work. I majored in sophomore English, by the way! And those words the pastor said to me lingered constantly in my mind: "You won't get this much in college," and he told me about the coming of the Lord Jesus Christ.

So I began to study about the second coming of Christ. And through these years I have delighted again and again and again at the blessed truth of the coming of our Saviour.

I am looking for Jesus to come. I believe in the bodily, imminent, personal, visible return of the Lord Jesus Christ back to this earth again. I believe the angels were right when they said, "Ye men of Galilee, why stand ye gazing up into heaven? this same Jesus, which is taken up from you into heaven, shall so come in like manner as ye have seen him go into heaven" (Acts 1:11).

I believe Jesus when He said, "I go to prepare a place for you. And if I go and prepare a place for you, I will come again, and receive you unto myself; that where I am there ye may be also" (John 14:2, 3).

And this doctrine has become a real, vital part of my ministry. And any church which is going to be a spiritual lighthouse for Christ must, of necessity, grasp this wonderful truth of the imminent return of our Saviour for His own. And I trust that you will make this a part of your life, and as we serve the Lord here together--whether it be for a long period or a short period--that we will make this constant looking for Christ to come in the clouds of glory a real, integral part of our church life and of our own personal life, for I believe He is going to come again.

And I hope you will understand this. I have gotten a reputation as being one of those preachers who emphasizes, maybe a little too much, the return of the Lord Jesus Christ. I have gotten that kind of reputation around the country, that I preach on the coming of the Lord Jesus Christ. Now when you get excited about something, it is rather difficult not to say something about it. As one of the secretaries said recently, "You know, you hardly ever get through a sermon without mentioning something about the coming of Christ."

I said, "Thank you."

She said, "What for?"

I said, "I appreciate the compliment."

I appreciated it, for He is going to come again, and He is going to catch some people, even some church members, unprepared and unaware. And since He is going to come again, I am duty-bound as a preacher of the Gospel of Christ to remind you of His coming.

Now I want to answer some questions that are always asked about the coming of Christ. Why all the fuss? What good does it do to look for Jesus to come? What does the Second Coming do for a child of God? What will it do for you to be looking for the coming of the Lord Jesus Christ in clouds of glory?

Suppose that you do get this thing in your life. Suppose that in your life it becomes a vital part, and every day you live expecting Jesus Christ to come at any moment. At any time Jesus could come in the clouds of glory and receive His saints up to Heaven to be with Him in the air. What should you do about it? He is going to come; what are Christians commanded in the Word of God to do about the coming of the Lord in the air?

There are several things we should do.

Preach His Coming

In the first place, we are commanded by God to preach on the second coming of the Lord Jesus Christ. In Titus, chapter 2, verses 13 through 15, it says that we are to look constantly for the blessed hope and the glorious appearing of our great God and Saviour, the Lord Jesus Christ. And he goes on down in verse 15 to say, "These things speak."

Now the book of Titus was written to a young preacher. Paul the aged was writing to one of his ministerial students, one of the young preachers, and Paul said, "Titus, always, always look for the blessed hope, the glorious appearing of our great God and our Saviour Jesus Christ." Then he said in verse 15, "Titus, these things speak." We have a command from God to preach on the return of the Lord Jesus Christ.

One of my favorite pastimes is reading biographies of great men. I read literally hundreds of biographies of men, over a hundred a year. Now I have read the biographies, I guess, of most of the great preachers of this generation and the last generation. By great, I mean men who have shaken the world for God. There is one great common denominator of all these great men and this is in every case, without exception, these men who had power with God have been men who have preached the second coming of the Lord Jesus Christ.

And so we are commanded to preach the coming of Jesus. You would be surprised how many Christians in America, born-again, God-fearing, Christ-loving people who know the Bible concerning His virgin birth, the new birth, the Bethlehem story, the life of Jesus Christ, the story of the epistles, the book of Acts, and other things in the Bible, how many hundreds and thousands of Christians who know all the rest of the Bible know little or nothing about this wonderful truth of the coming of our Saviour in the air. The reason is, we have silenced our pulpits on preaching about the return of Christ. This is not part of my message, but I throw it in. Many churches, many denominations, and many preachers have taken certain Bible truths and have perverted them.

You take on the subject of the Holy Spirit, the baptism of the Holy Ghost, the subject of speaking in other tongues, and other doctrines of the Bible, and this also, the doctrine of the coming of Jesus Christ--many have perverted it. Date-setters, time-setters, people who spend too much time among the signs and less time on the coming; chart drawers (I am not criticising all the chart drawers, but those who are only chart drawers); people who read the book of Revelation like a mathematics book instead of a love story, people who have perverted the doctrine, have made many of us Baptists shy away from preaching the return of our Lord Jesus Christ. But I am not going to, shall I say, cheat you out of this wonderful doctrine. I trust it will be a part of you. And so I am commanded to preach it.

Two preachers were talking. One was a preacher who believed the coming of Christ. One did not. One preacher said to the other, "The difference in you and me is that I just don't preach on the coming of Christ and you do."

The other preacher answered quickly, "No sir. That isn't the difference in you and me. The difference is that I am doing what God said to do, and you are not."

God plainly said to young preachers, "These things speak." We must of necessity preach about the coming of the Lord Jesus.

The second thing we are to do concerning our attitude toward His coming is that we are to

Look for His Coming.

Hebrews 9:28 says, "...unto them that look for him shall he appear the second time without sin unto salvation." To them that what? To them that look. That word look is an interesting word. It means gaze, actually gaze. We constantly look for the coming of Christ.

My Bible says, "...unto them that look for him [to them that gaze for him; to them that gaze in the sky for him; to them that look constantly, expectantly, lovingly, wishfully toward the skies, look behind every cloud to see if Jesus is behind that cloud] shall he appear the second time without sin unto salvation." Unto them that look for him!

Bishop Steed was a dear preacher of yesterday. The last thing he did before retiring in the evening was to go to his window, lift up the shade, raise the window, and look up to see if Jesus was coming. The first thing he did in the morning upon rising was to go to the window, lift the shade, raise the window, and look out to see if Jesus was coming that morning. It was a vital part of his life.

I dare you to start looking for Christ to come. I dare you to make it a vital part of your life. Do you want your life to be clean and pure? Do you want to give up some sins? Do you want to go to places that would honor the Lord Jesus Christ? Do you want to watch what you read? Do you want to be careful about your habits? Do you want to be careful about the things you do, the places you go? Then you make it your habit to do what the Bible says. Look, gaze longingly upward toward the coming of the Lord Jesus Christ. We are to look for His coming.

You and I recall when we were little children. Daddy would leave in the morning. I had a big, husky daddy--5 feet and 14 inches, I believe he was! He used to be a professional wrestler and he could whip anybody. I just knew he could. I would watch him leave in the morning, then long for him to come in the afternoon. When Daddy came home I would be looking for him. I didn't understand how to tell time. I didn't know exactly what time Dad was coming. So about the time he usually came in, after I woke from my afternoon nap, I would begin to look down the sidewalk. I would look for him constantly.

Then I would see him come around the corner. I can see him now, on Oak Cliff Boulevard in Dallas. As he came around the corner I would run lickety split with my little bare feet down the hot sidewalk and jump up in Daddy's arms, and say, "Daddy, it's good to have you.... What did you bring me! What did you bring me, Daddy?" For when I knew his coming was near, I began to look constantly for Daddy to come home.

The same is true with the Lord Jesus Christ. What are we supposed to do? Look! We are supposed to keep our eyes Heavenward. Everyday it should be a part of your life to look up and think of the coming of the Lord Jesus Christ. What if it were today!

Now then, there is something else we are to do. We are to preach it, we are to look for it, and in the third place, we are to

Pray for His Coming.

> "Our Father which art in heaven, Hallowed be thy name. Thy kingdom come...."

What does that mean? "Come back, Jesus, and establish Your kingdom. We are tired of running this world without You."

I noticed that Rockefeller has decided not to run for Vice-President. Lots of fellows are going to decide not to run for President, I have an idea! I noticed that the great conventions are about to come, and sides are taking form, and the elections are about to come off, and nominations are about here. Oh, the excitement it has generated! These same people, if they came to church and one little fellow let out one little grunt of an "amen," they would say, "He is getting fanatical. A screw loose there. He ought not do that in the church house."

The same crowd! The same ones! They will get a banner and get in a dignified Democratic convention and march around, "WE WANT KENNEDY! WE WANT KENNEDY!" And you come to church, and if the preacher hollers half that loud you think he has lost his mind. We can't get as excited over Jesus Christ and His coming kingdom as we can over the White House occupant the next four years in our own country.

I am saying, when God's people get as excited over the kingdom of Jesus Christ as they do over Eisenhower and Kennedy and Symington and Humphrey and Nixon--if we get as excited about the coming King and we look for Him, long for Him, even pray for Him--people in America will believe what we preach and believe what we say we believe. Our country is dying for Christians who will constantly feel as citizens of Christ's Kingdom and pray, "Thy kingdom come."

Revelation 22:17 is very interesting. I have preached on it many times. It says:

> "And the Spirit and the bride say, Come. And let him that heareth say, Come. And let him that is athirst come. And whosoever will, let him take the water of life freely."

Now, that verse means, of course, that the Spirit of God says, "Come to Jesus," and the bride says, "Come to Jesus," and those who hear say, "Come to Jesus." But I remind you of this: The book of Revelation is a prophetic book, a book about the second coming of Jesus Christ. And when we close the book in Revelation 22:20, "Even so, come, Lord Jesus" it means this: "The Holy Spirit says, 'Come, Jesus.' The bride says, 'Come, Jesus.' Him that heareth says, 'Come, Jesus.'" We join that great heavenly chant, an earthly chant constantly saying, "Come, Comc, Come, Jesus!" And that is what we are supposed to do--pray for the coming of our Saviour.

About the time a touchdown is about to be scored on the ten-yard line at a football game, the cheerleaders get those big megaphones and start shouting, "Go! Go! Go!" Before long the band is drumming the same thing. The bass drum is hitting it and the band is chanting it, "Go! Go! Go!" Then the student body--"Go! Go! Go!" Then all the fans--"Go! Go! Go!" Finally it rings over the field and echoes across the land--"Go! Go!" Why? They are anxious for a touchdown.

Wouldn't it be wonderful if God's people could get as excited about Christianity as they can about scoring a touchdown on the football field? Wouldn't that be wonderful? What we ought to do, the Bible says, is shout, "The Spirit says, Come. And the Bride says, Come. And him that heareth says, Come. Whosoever will, join in and say, Come! Come!" The very heartbeat of the Christian ought to be for the Lord Jesus Christ, "Come on from Heaven, Jesus. Come back and get me. This old sin-cursed world, this old world of pain and sorrow and sickness and death and heartache and bereavement and heartbreak--come back and get me; come back and receive me! Come back and take me home to Heaven." That ought to be the constant chant of every born-again child of God. "Come."

And so we ought to pray for His coming. We should preach it; we should look for it; we should pray for it. John closes the Bible with the last prayer in the Word of God by saying, "Even so, come, Lord Jesus."

Now the last prayer in the Bible is not, "Now I lay me down to sleep...."

As the fellow said, "I bet you a dollar you can't quote the Lord's Prayer."

The other old boy said, "I will take you up. I bet you a dollar I can."

Then the other said, "Okay, try it."

He said, "Now I lay me down to sleep; I pray the Lord my soul to keep...."

This other fellow said, "Okay, you win! You win!"

Now the last prayer in the Bible is not the Lord's Prayer. The last prayer in the Bible is not, "Now I lay me down to sleep...." The last prayer in the Bible is not praying for the Holy Ghost. The last prayer in the Bible is not praying for daily bread. The last prayer in the Bible is not praying for strength in temptation. But the last concluding prayer in the Bible is this prayer: "Even so, come, Lord Jesus."

We are commanded to pray for His coming.

We should preach it; we should look for it; we should pray for it; then we should

Love It.

In II Timothy, chapter 4, verses 7 and 8, Paul said:

> "I have fought a good fight, I have finished my course, I have kept the faith: Henceforth there is laid up for me a crown of righteousness, which the Lord, the righteous judge, shall give me at that day: and not to me only, but unto all them also that love his appearing."

"To all them that love his appearing." Paul said, "Timothy, I am about to be delivered. My fight is over; my course is run. I have kept the faith. Now I am going to receive my eternal, heavenly rewards. But," he said, "I am going to get a crown of righteousness." And he said, "Timothy, you can have one too, if you love His appearing." "Love his appearing."

There are two words in the Bible for love. One is phileo, which means like you love to eat; you love to sleep; you love to come to church; you love to take a nap; you love to rest; you love to read a book. That is the word phileo. It means filial love, harmless. But there is another word in the Bible for love, which is the word agape. The word agape means deep love, yearning love, heart love, heartthrob, heartbeat love, and that is the word in II Timothy, chapter 4, verse 8. "...unto all them also that agape his appearing." "...unto all them also that love deeply in their soul His appearing."

Now many of you love His appearing bodily. It would be okay with you. You wouldn't mind. Of course you would rather wait until after you buy that new dress or that new suit or get your new car. You don't mind His coming. It is okay with you if the preacher wants to get up and holler about it. You don't mind; you will tolerate it. You accept it, and it is all right to preach about it because the Bible says it, but you are not going to get excited about it. The Bible commands that we love deeply--a yearning, abiding love for the coming of the Lord Jesus Christ.

Oh, how we love to take parts of the Bible and leave the

rest out. We love to take John 3:16 and say we are fundamental. But we are not truly fundamental until we love the appearing of the Lord Jesus Christ, for in loving His appearing, we have laid up for ourselves a crown of righteousness just like the Apostle Paul received.

What does it mean to love His appearing? You recall those days in World War II, don't you? Your loved one was overseas. There was nothing but a picture on the mantel... a star in the window...a few memories...a letter occasionally. You wondered day after day if he were going to live.

Finally the good news came. Oh, I will never forget that day the war was over! I was on maneuvers. I was out in dirty old grimy maneuvers, with mud all over my face, shooting on the rifle range, and in the 82nd Airborne Division making parachute jumps. We were way, way out on maneuvers, away out, away from anybody. Finally a jeep came out. The fellow shouted, "Extra! Extra! War is over! War is over! Japan has surrendered!"

Ah, brother! You talk about wonderful, wonderful things! Sweaty! (that's perspiration) and dirty and filthy and big old husky men needing a shave for a week and way out in the woods! Do you know what we did? You would have thought we loved each other dearly! We hugged. We kissed. I even hugged the Second Lieutenant, and that takes a great deal of love! I hugged him--I did! I went up to the Colonel, and for the first time in my life I had the biggest joy of my life; I took his cap and messed it up. War is over!

Oh, you took that picture on the mantel and you looked at it and said, "Now he can come home!" Little children began to say, "Daddy is coming home!" Mothers said, "Son is coming home!" Sweethearts said, "He is coming home!" Wives said, "Husband is coming home!" The ships were full of the chants of hurry! Every day you waited, you could hardly wait for the day to come. Every moment of your life you lived for him to come home.

And then the day happened. It took place. He came! You met him! He was home! The thrill! You loved his appearing.

And that is what Jesus means. Our lives should be consumed with loving the appearing of our wonderful Saviour. He is coming some day. The clouds of glory shall break open and the Saviour will come for His bride, to take us as a spotless church and present us spotlessly before the throne of the Heavenly Father. Every day we should say, "Come! Come! Come!"

Tomorrow morning when you get up, why don't you say, "Is He going to come today?" Tomorrow night when you go to bed, why don't you say, "Jesus, come tonight while I am asleep." The next morning when you wake up say, "Jesus, come today." And love it, agape-like love, not phileo love, but deep, abiding, yearning love, begging for the Saviour to come again.

Our attitude toward His coming--to preach it, to look for it, to pray for it, to love it; and then we ought to be

Comforted by His Coming.

What a wonderful chapter is I Thessalonians, chapter 4, where it says:

> "...the dead in Christ shall rise first: Then we which are alive and remain shall be caught up together with them in the clouds, to meet the Lord in the air: and so shall we ever be with the Lord."

The entire story of the program of His coming is told in I Thessalonians, chapter 4, verses 13 through 17, and in closing the Lord says, "Wherefore comfort one another with these words."

"Comfort one another with these words." Don't misunderstand me and don't be critical of this statement. But I think along here somewhere we Christians need some growth in grace. We have the idea that comfort nowadays is some soft, soothing, hopeless, helpless word from someone with a saddened personality.

For example, you are in bed sick, desperately ill. I come and I say, "Mr.____, may the Heavenly Father be near to you."

That is what we call comfort. That is all right, but I know something better. I can say, "Mr.____, Jesus may come and take you out of this place." And the Bible says that is real comfort.

If you want to comfort somebody who is about to die, you tell him Jesus may come before he dies. That is comfort.

Do you want to comfort those who have laid a loved one in the grave and they walk away with the heavens turned to brass and their hearts are empty and their lives forsaken and it seems as if nobody cares? You tell them that grave is going to open some day and their loved one will come out of the grave. The bereaved will find real comfort in that.

You want to comfort somebody some time who has a serious illness, you remind him that when Jesus comes in clouds of glory and all the holy angels with Him, there will be no pain; there will be no suffering; there will be no sorrow; there will be no heartache; there will be no funeral homes; there will be no hearses; there will be no handkerchiefs; there will be no tombstones; there will be no caskets or coffins. Comfort one another with these words.

No use to look to die when Jesus is going to come. A famous preacher who was dying always said that Jesus was going to come in his lifetime. As he was dying someone came to his bedside and said, "They say you are dying."

He said, "You tell them they are lying. You tell them they are lying."

"What do you mean?"

He said, "I am looking for Jesus to come, and I believe He is going to come back before I pass on."

That is what I mean. Comfort one another with these words.

We are to preach it; we are to look for it; we are to pray for it; to love it; to be comforted by it; then may I say, in closing, we are to

Be Prepared for His Coming.

In I John, chapter 3, verses 1 through 3, it says:

> "Behold, what manner of love the Father hath bestowed upon us, that we should be called the sons of God...it doth not yet appear what we shall be: but we know that, when he shall appear, we shall be like him; for we shall see him as he is. And every man that hath this hope in him purifieth himself, even as he is pure."

The reason some of you folks have dirty lives is because you are not looking for Christ to come. The reason some of you young people have in your album, records that are filthy and sexy and vulgar is because you do not realize that Jesus Christ could come while you are playing those records. The reason some of you men have some pictures where you work of ladies posed immodestly is because you are not looking for Jesus Christ to come and find pictures like that on your wall. The reason some of you ladies have those True Stories and Modern Romances and Confidential magazines tucked away in your library where the preacher can't see them is because you do not realize that Jesus Christ might come back while you are reading that trash. The reason some of you friends go out on the dance floor is because you do not realize that Jesus Christ could come again while you are in the arms of somebody else's wife or husband. The reason many, many, many of our ladies clothe themselves immodestly is because they are not looking for Jesus to come.

My precious friends, when we get our eyes upon the heavens and realize that in any moment the shout, the trump of God, the voice of the archangel could break up the heavens, the graves could open, the dead in Christ could rise and Jesus Christ could find us at any moment doing any given thing, it would change our lives completely and help us to purify our lives for Jesus' sake.

Do you know why I come to church on Sunday night? I would not want Jesus to come on Sunday night and not find me in church. Do you know one reason why I come to church on Wednesday night? Because I would not want Jesus to come and find me at home watching the prize fight while somebody is teaching Revelation down here at the church house. Wouldn't you be embarrassed if Jesus came next Wednesday night while you were watching Dynamite Gun knock out Joe Paluka, and the Bible was being taught at the church house?

Oh, my soul hungers tonight for real Bible Christianity where people are looking for the coming of our blessed Lord. Go ahead and say what you want to say. Call me a fanatic; call me a nut; call me a nit-wit; call me crazy; but I am telling you the reason the world laughs at us Christians is because it knows we are not dedicated to our task of serving Christ.

Mahatma Gandhi could have turned a third of the world to Christ. If he had been converted, he could have turned the greatest percentage of heathen people to Christ of any man who has lived in our generation. Mahatma Gandhi made this statement: "I would have become a Christian had it not been for Christians."

Dr. J. B. Lawrence has said, "We don't need more Baptists; we need better Baptists, for when we get better Baptists, we will have more Baptists."

I am looking today for His glorious appearing. My precious friends, some of you have things in your life which you are not going to give up. You don't like the idea of some little preacher pointing his finger in your face and telling you about your sins. But, thank God, some will. You have some sins in your life that are a reproach to Jesus Christ. And tonight you ought to say, "By God's grace, I believe He could come at any moment, and I don't want Jesus to come and find me doing something that will be a reproach to the Gospel of Christ and the blessed Word of God." We ought to prepare for His coming.

A famous feudal lord years ago had what we call a fool. Back in those days they called them comedian fools. Every feudal estate--the old manor form of government and life--every feudal estate had to have a comedian. They called him a fool.

One day the lord of an estate called his fool in and said, "Fool, I believe you are the biggest fool I have ever seen. Here, take my rod and circle the world and see if you can find a bigger fool than yourself. If you find a bigger one, give my rod to that fool. But if you return after your trip around the world and still have the rod, I will know that you are the biggest fool of all."

This comedian, this fool, began his trip. He looked around the world for comedians, fools, bigger than himself, but he was the biggest fool of all. Finally he returned to his lord. He still had the rod. He walked into the estate. Someone told him his lord was seriously ill. He walked into the lord's room; the lord was sick unto death. The doctor said he could not live. The fool walked in, rod in hand, and said, "My lord, someone said you are ill."

"That is right," he said. "Fool, I am going to go. I am going to take a trip."

Whereupon the fool replied, "Are you ready to take a trip?"

The lord looked at the fool and said, "Fool, I am not ready to take the trip! I am going to go, but I am not ready!"

As the fool looked at him, he placed the rod in the hands

of the lord and said, "Here, lord, if you are going to die and are not ready, you are the biggest fool of all."

My precious friends, if Christ is going to come, if He is going to come again and we are not ready for His coming, we are the biggest fools of all. I am so happy that if Jesus Christ blows the trumpet tonight and the dead in Christ shall rise, I too, would rise to meet Him in the air.

What should our attitude be toward His coming? We should love His coming; we should look for His coming; we should preach His coming; we should be comforted by His coming; we should pray for His coming; and we should prepare for the coming of our Saviour.

May I ask you a question? Suppose Jesus had come back last night at ten o'clock. Think! Suppose Jesus had come back last night at ten o'clock. Think where you were. Would you have been happy for Jesus to come last night at ten?

Suppose Jesus Christ were to come back this Wednesday night at seven thirty. Would you be pleased for Him to find you where you were last Wednesday night? Suppose Jesus Christ were to come back and find you in those places where you have been going. I am simply saying this: We should live every day so that Jesus would be pleased if He came and found us in our condition presently.

I am looking today for His glorious appearing. I keep scanning the skies, for the promise is nigh. I am looking today for Him.

Let us bow our heads in prayer. Our heads are bowed; our eyes are closed. Would you open your heart to Him? Would some of you break down the wall of resistance and barrier? Would you open your heart tonight? How many of you will say, "Preacher, I have some things in my life that I would be ashamed for Jesus to find me doing when He comes again. I will have to admit, there are some things that I do, some places I go, some things I read, some words I say, some music I hear, or some things that I do not do that I should be doing, but I would be ashamed for Christ to come and find me in that condition"? How many of you will be honest tonight?

I am not trying to hurt you. I am not against you. I love you. I want you to be pleased when Jesus comes. I want you to have the joy of being ready and prepared for His coming. I wouldn't hurt you. I have no desire in this world to take a sermon and hit you in the head with it and say, "I got you back." I have no desire for that, not a bit. But, oh, if I could cause some to prepare for His coming; if by God's mercy and by God's grace some would forsake some sins and say, "Preacher, tonight pray for me. There is something in my life I would be ashamed if Jesus came and found me doing it. I tonight want you to pray for me." I wonder if you would lift your hand? God bless you! Oh, yes! God bless all of you.

But there are many of you tonight--you know who you are --you know that when a preacher points his finger across the pulpit, you rebel. You don't want any preacher telling you what to do. You don't want anybody reminding you of your sins. Oh, listen! We are on the same side tonight. We are trying to get a job done for God. I am trying to help you. I am trying to lead you to a closer life. Who else will say, "Include me in the prayer. There are some things I would be ashamed for Christ to find me doing, and I want you to pray for me, too"? Lift your hands. Oh, God bless you, and you, and you.

PRAYER

Our Father, we ask for those who wanted prayer. Now we pray. We want our church to be clean; we want our people to be separated; we want our people to love God, love the Bible, love the things of God. We want our people not to love the world nor the things of the world. The Bible says, "Whosoever loveth the world, the love of the Father is not in him." We want our people to love spiritual things, and the things of God. So tonight, we pray that You will bless the lives of these precious friends--many young people, many new Christians, many children. We pray that You would help them. And when the trumpet does sound, we pray that You will help us to be found faithful. So it can be said of us as it was said of the apostle, "I have fought a good fight, I have finished the course, I have kept the faith: Henceforth there is laid up for me a crown of righteousness." We pray we may be able to say that.

While our heads are bowed, if tonight you have never received Christ; if tonight you have never been born by the Spirit of God; if tonight you have never come to the place in your life where you have turned from sin and turned to Jesus, and Christ came tonight, your chances of salvation would be gone. There are some tonight who ought to walk the aisles of this church and receive Christ as Saviour. There are some of you who should come and present yourself for church membership. We hope you will do it. May God help you to do it tonight.

Father, bless the invitation, in the name of Christ. Amen.

Burning Messages for the Unsaved

7

To Hell and Back

Tonight I close the series of messages on the Second Coming by giving a rather detailed Bible study on the subject of Hell. Now I will not necessarily preach an evangelistic sermon; rather, I would like to acquaint you with Hell and explain exactly what the Bible teaches about it, using twenty-two different verses of Scripture. Rather than look them up, perhaps I could quote them, or give you the references as I bring the message, and you make a note in the margin of your Bible, or on a piece of paper as to what the Bible says about Hell, then you may have them for future references.

There are three worlds in existence. The world about us here who live on this earth. Then there is the world about which we spoke this morning. I always like to preach something about Heaven close to the time when I preach on Hell, because invariably somebody will nip at me and say that all I do is preach on wrath, Hell, and judgment. So I preach on Heaven to balance it off.

I will teach awhile tonight, with a little preaching interspersed, on the subject, "To Hell and Back." Actually the Bible teaches that people do go to Hell and come back.

The Bible has a great deal to say about Hell. In fact, it has more to say about Hell than about Heaven. There are more Scriptures in the Bible that teach about Hell than teach about Heaven; there are more verses in the Bible which tell about the conditions of Hell than you find telling about the conditions of Heaven. Now for a person to close his eyes on the subject of Hell is to refuse to believe a portion of the Word of God.

Modern scholarship says, "There is no such thing as Hell." For example:

Dr. DeHaan, the famous radio preacher, had preached many years ago on the subject of Hell on the radio. Some preacher--I say preacher--"reverend"--wrote him and in these words he said:

"Dear Dr. DeHaan:

"I am surprised that a man of your training and background, from college, university, and seminary, could believe in that antiquated, moth-eaten, disproved theory of the age of superstition that there is a literal Hell. No modern scholar believes that any longer."

Well, no modern scholar believed the flood was coming either, but it came. No modern scholar believed that Sodom and Gomorrah would be destroyed, but it was. In fact, all the modern scholars were destroyed with them.

Don't misunderstand me; I believe in education. It seems I spent all my life in school. I spent eighteen years hunting the "x" in algebra! I never found it, but I spent eighteen years hunting for it! I hate to disillusion you, but it ain't there! You can't find it! I believe in education. I believe in study. I believe in reading. I read three and a half books last week. Usually I read three to five books a week. I believe in study. But I want to say that if modern scholarship does not believe the Bible, modern scholarship can go down the garbage can of human history as far as I am concerned. I am going to believe the Word of God. And a fellow who is an educated person but who does not believe the Bible, is just an educated fool. I would rather be a little fellow who had never seen the inside of a school, and believe the Bible is the Word of God, and be born again and love God and love the Word of God and believe the Bible and what God says in the Bible, than to be a man with all the degrees a mile long and not be able to understand and believe the Word of God.

There is no truth without the One who says, "I am the Truth." And when you get to the place in your life where you think you are too modern for this Bible, you are too modern for God and you will go to Hell like all the other scholars will who do not believe the Word of God.

The Bible is very plain. You will have to decide one or two things: whether you do not believe the Bible, or you believe in Hell, because if you believe the Bible, you have to believe in Hell. A lot of people would say, "I don't believe in a burning Hell. I don't believe that folks who die in their sins burn forever." You do not believe the Bible then. "Oh, yes, I believe the Bible." No you don't. If you don't believe there is a Hell, if you don't believe there is a burning Hell, you do not believe the Bible is the Word of God, for the Bible is very clear about this matter. We will discuss many Scriptures tonight that will leave no doubt in any Bible-believer's mind about the truth and the doctrine of an eternal, literal, burning Hell-fire where people who die in their sins must spend eternity and must live forever without God.

Several years ago Audie Murphy, I think the most decorated of all the World War II heroes, wrote a book entitled To Hell and Back. Audie Murphy likened World War II to Hell. He told about the men whose heads were disengaged from their bodies; about the men who were mangled; about seeing horror and death and bloodshed and mangled bodies, the torn battlefields and all the horrors of World War II. Then in coming back--he likened that as to coming back from Hell. So he titled the book, To Hell and Back.

Audie Murphy had an awful time in World War II. My heart certainly goes out to all those who suffer in all wars, and who give their lives and their health and many times the members of their bodies for our lives. But may I say this, my precious friends: World War II, World War I, the coming World War III, the Battle of Armageddon and all the rest of them, will never have one little iota compared to the suffering of Hell-fire where the worm dieth not and the fire is not quenched.

I will give you Bible facts about Hell tonight. I will not

say one thing in this pulpit tonight unless it is authenticated by the Word of God.

I. HELL'S REASON, LOCATION, PROPHECY, AND DURATION

The first thing I would call your attention to is

The Reason for Hell.

In Matthew 25:41 the Bible says, "Then shall he say also unto them on the left hand, Depart from me, ye cursed, into everlasting fire, prepared for the devil and his angels."

What is the purpose for Hell? Why was Hell made? Often children ask that question.

One little girl asked her mother one day, "Mother, what does the world rest on? What does the world rest on?"

The mother didn't know what the world rested on any more than the child did. So she said, "Oh, the world rests on er...er...er...on a big man...a big man. A big man holds the world up." Then she went about her business.

"Mama, what does the man stand on?"

"Oh, honey, the man stands on a...a...a...a...oh, he stands on a big...a big rock. That is what the man stands on."

"Mama, what does the rock sit on?"

"Oh, the rock sits on a big pole. A great big long pole."

"Mama, what does the pole sit on?"

"Ah, hush, honey! The pole just goes all the way down to the bottom."

Now many boys and girls have many questions to ask. Many have asked me this question, "Brother Hyles, why was Hell made? What is Hell for? Who made Hell? Why was Hell prepared in the first place?" So I will discuss with you the reason for Hell. There was a reason.

Before the world was ever created, before there ever was an earth, a Mars, a Jupiter, a Venus; before there ever was a sun, or moon, or stars, there was a Heaven. God lived in the Heaven, in fellowship with His angels. It is thought there were three different companies of angels under three different archangels, Gabriel, Michael, and Lucifer, who is the Devil. Three different (you might say) battalions or regiments of angels. Now Lucifer decided he wanted to take over Heaven, so Lucifer rebelled against God and took his group of the angels and started a war in Heaven. Immediately God put down the rebellion of Lucifer, and cast him and his angels out of Heaven. They were excommunicated from Heaven.

If that be so, immediately God prepared a place for the Devil and these angels, Heaven's fallen angels and the Devil. The place was called Hell. In Matthew 25:41 it says they were cast into everlasting fire "prepared for the devil and his angels." As I have said many times, if you go to Hell, you will be an intruder. Hell was not made for you. But if you do not receive Christ, you will go there, and you will burn forever. I don't care how many degrees you have; I don't care how smart you are; I don't care how rich you are; I don't care how influential you are; you will go to Hell and you will burn forever unless you have been born again. So Hell is a place made for the Devil and his angels.

Let me tell you something. I get a little sick sometimes with certain classes of people. The only thing I can't stand in this world is prejudice. This idea that there are two kinds of preachers--the Hell-fire-and-brimstone preacher, and then there is the educated kind. The Devil thought that up. "There is that Hell-fire-and-brimstone preacher, the kind that hangs you over Hell. Then there is the kinder, sweeter type." Let me tell you something, if you are going to Hell and a fellow doesn't tell you about it, he isn't sweet; he is the biggest enemy you have! If a world is lost without God, if a world is headed for damnation forever, to live in the fires of an eternal torment forever, and a man stands in a pulpit and some of his people are headed for Hell, and that man does not tell them about Hell, he is the worst enemy they have. I don't care how sweet he is, or how kind. The best friend you have, the sweetest preacher who stands in anybody's pulpit is the one who reminds you to escape the fires of Hell, for there is a prepared place for unprepared people somewhere, where people suffer in the world to come forever and forever. The reason for Hell.

In the second place I call your attention to

The Location of Hell.

Where is Hell? People are always asking me. Where is Hell located? How do you go there? In what part of the universe is Hell? I am not sure about that except to say this: the Bible seems to imply that Hell is down. Usually in the Bible when Heaven is mentioned, it is up, and when mentioning Hell, it is going down. So Hell must be down. I personally believe that Hell is in the heart of the earth. I believe that future Gehenna, Hell will be in the heart of the earth. Scientists say that beneath the earth there is a boiling volcanic disturbance constantly going on in the heart of the earth. And so I personally believe Hell will be in the heart of the earth.

Now then, Hell is also called "a bottomless pit." In Revelation 9:2 it says the angel "opened the bottomless pit; and there arose a smoke out of the pit, as the smoke of a great furnace...." A bottomless pit.

My precious friend, you can be a Baptist, you can be a Methodist, you can be a Presbyterian, you can be a Catholic, you can be an Episcopalian, you can be a Lutheran and all the rest of them; you can be baptized in this pool, and sprinkled in another church, and confirmed in another, and reared in another, but if you die without Jesus Christ, without being born again, the Bible says you will go to Hell and suffer in a bottomless pit.

I believe in Hell people constantly fall forever and forever. There is no bottom to Hell. It is a bottomless pit. While people are burning, they shall also be falling. While people are screaming and crying and begging for mercy, and pleading for water, and while they are gnashing their teeth, and chewing their tongues, and looking to God and saying, "O God! Send Lazarus that he may dip his finger in water and cool my tongue, for I am tormented in this flame"--the Bible says that is a bottomless pit. Constant falling! Constant falling! Again and again; no foundation, no rock, nothing to stand upon--a bottomless pit forever and forever and forever!

In World War II, I was in the paratroopers. I made nineteen parachute jumps or "push-outs"! I know what it is to fall. On my fifth parachute jump, my parachute did not open. One hundred feet from the ground...one second from death, my reserve parachute finally opened. I know what it is to fall. I fell seven hundred feet in the air. I twisted. I did not know whether my head was up or down. My arms were completely uncontrollable. I could not hold my body with any co-ordination at all. I was just falling and twisting in the air, just completely unco-ordinated...falling...falling...falling; turning...turning; twisting...twisting.

Think of it. In Hell--a bottomless pit. Forever and forever! Falling and burning and crying and twisting in a bottomless pit forever!

The location of Hell is a bottomless pit, which I believe is down.

We have seen the reason for Hell; we have seen the location of Hell; now I call your attention to

The Prophecy of Hell.

In the Bible it plainly teaches that people can go to Hell and get out. In fact, people who are in Hell tonight will get out someday.

I am not talking about the person going to purgatory and if he gets enough prayers and enough money paid for him, he can get on up to the next place. I am talking about the fact that people who are in Hell shall some day be discharged from Hell. Here is why.

Revelation 20:13, 14 says this: "And the sea gave up the dead which were in it; and death and hell delivered up the dead which were in them: and they were judged every man according to their works. And death and hell were cast into the lake of fire."

Ken (our song leader), I will use you for an example. You be in Hell for a minute. The place where you are sitting represents Hell. It is torment, constant soul-torment. But in Hell tonight the soul-torment is all there is. The body is not tormented in Hell tonight, but just the soul. The body of the lost man goes to the grave; the soul goes to Hades or what is commonly called now Hell. The soul goes to torment.

Now John (assistant pastor), you be the body of an unsaved person. Ken is the soul. The soul is in Hades burning; the body is in the grave. Now one day, at the resurrection of the unsaved, at the end of the thousand-year millennium, the soul shall come out of Hell, the body shall come out of the grave and body and soul shall be reunited, for Hell now is only disembodied spirits. But in that day it shall be embodied spirits, and the body and soul shall be together again, and both body and soul shall stand before God at the great judgment that Ken sang about a bit ago, they will stand before God and He will give them degrees of punishment in the lake of fire, and every one of them will be cast again, both body and soul, back into the lake of fire to be tormented forever and forever.

So the soul which is in Hell tonight will come out of Hell, and be delivered for awhile, just for a moment as it stands before God and then God will take body and soul and cast them into the lake of fire.

That word "cast" in the Greek is a very interesting word. It is the word ekballo, which means to hurl as you would hurl a ball or throw a rock. In the Bible when someone would throw something, as a rock or stone, it was ekballo. They would hurl it, throw it. And that word "cast" in Revelation 20:14 actually means people shall be taken both body and soul and shall be thrown into the lake of fire.

I tremble when I think about these preachers standing before God one day and He looks at them and says, "My Bible was full of Scriptures about Hell and you were afraid to tell them about Hell. You had some educated folks, and you were afraid to tell them about Hell. You had some folks who thought Hell wasn't true, and you cut your message, you trimmed the corners." Woe be unto any preacher who stands before his people and for fear of preaching something the folks don't like, he fails to warn them of the wrath of God to come!

There is going to be a time when the body shall come from the grave and the soul shall come from Hades, and body and soul together shall be hurled into the lake of fire. Like it or not, it is there. It is in the Bible. If you don't believe it, it is still in the Bible. The Bible is clear about the prophecy of Hell.

We have seen the reason for Hell, we have seen the location of Hell, we have seen the prophecy of Hell; now I would have you notice

The Duration of Hell.

How long is Hell? What is the duration? I believe in purgatory, but not the purgatory that some of our friends believe in. The Bible says in Hebrews that Jesus purged our sins on the tree. And if you want to know what the Bible says there, in the original language it says He purgatoried our sins. It is the same word as purgatory. Jesus purgatoried our sins. On the cross of Calvary, Jesus Christ suffered and purged our sins for us.

Consequently, we who are in Him will not go to purgatory, and those who are out of Him have not had their sins purged already, and so Hell will be forever. In Revelation 14:11 it says, "And the smoke of their torment ascendeth up for ever and ever...."

Go home tonight, turn on your kitchen stove, put your

finger in the fire, hold it there ten minutes, and see what you pull out. You go home tonight, you put your finger in the fire, you hold it five minutes, just five minutes, then see what you pull out.

"Oh," you say, "I wouldn't do that."

Okay; what about four?

"Why," you say, "I am not that big enough fool."

How about three?

"Why," you say, "preacher, you are foolish."

How about two?

"Why," you say, "I still am not going...."

How about one?

"Why," you say, "you are crazy."

All right, how about ten seconds then? We will leave the minutes off. How about ten seconds?

"Why," you say, "preacher, I wouldn't pull back anything but a stub."

Well, how about five seconds? Turn the fire on, you put your finger in the kitchen fire one...two...three...four... five seconds--see what you pull out.

You say, "I won't do it."

Well, how about four seconds? How about three? How about two? How about one? How about putting your finger in the fire and saying, "One second,"--pull it out?

No, you wouldn't do it. Yet my friends, Hell is longer than one second! Hell is longer than two seconds! Hell is longer than five seconds! Hell is longer than ten seconds! Hell is longer than ten minutes! Hell is longer than ten days! Hell is longer than ten weeks! Hell is longer than ten months! Hell is longer than ten years! Hell is longer than ten thousand years! Hell is longer than ten million years! Hell is longer than ten billion years! Hell is longer than ten trillion years! There are many people who would not be so foolish as for one single second to put their finger in the fire of the kitchen stove, yet who are plunging their souls toward a place of torment where they will burn for millions and billions of years forever, without hope in the world to come! Oh, think of it! Hell is eternal. It never ceases. The duration of Hell!

We have seen the reason for Hell, the location of Hell, the prophecy of Hell, the duration of Hell; now we come lastly to

II. THE SUFFERINGS OF HELL

We will spend most of our time tonight on the sufferings of Hell. I don't want anybody to go to Hell. God knows I don't. And I want to make this clear. If I did not believe in Hell, I would get out of this business. If I did not believe in Hell, I would close my Bible and not preach another sermon. If I did not believe that people who are lost and die without God will burn forever, I would close my Bible and get in some lucrative profession and I would get as much out of life as possible. I would say the Epicureans are right: I will live and eat and drink and be merry, for tomorrow I die. Because I believe in Hell, the motivating power of my ministry is the fact that I believe people to whom I preach may go to Hell.

Sometimes I am criticized for being evangelistic all the time. Many times people say, "Why don't you give the Christians more?" I do try to give the Christians more. The crowd that thinks I don't give the Christians enough is the crowd that doesn't come back on Sunday night or Wednesday night. I try to give Christians something. But there is always that constant inner motivating power that people to whom I preach on Sunday morning and Sunday night and Wednesday night are eternity-bound people headed somewhere, and some of them will live forever in the place of the unprepared.

Oh, as I have preached sermon after sermon after sermon, and many people have heard me preach and have not been saved, and they have plunged their way toward Hell, they have died without hearing the Gospel again; I stop and think there are people tonight burning while I am preaching tonight; they are screaming while I am preaching tonight; they are in Hell, falling in the bottomless pit, gnashing their teeth, in darkness forever and ever and ever and ever! How in the name of good common sense can any man who calls himself a preacher of God's Gospel help but warn people about the wrath of God to come is more than I can understand.

I promised God years ago that I would be the kind of a preacher to preach all the Bible. I promised Him that nobody would change it. I promised God that no one would influence my preaching but Him. If you want to make me real mad, where I tell you to sit back where you belong, you just try to tell me what to preach. Oh, you will have your hands full! You really will! You can tell me my tie isn't straight, and I will try to straighten it up. You can tell me that my suit isn't exactly the right color, and I will try to buy a new one. But you leave my preaching alone. That is between me and God.

I want to say this tonight: the Bible plainly teaches that there is a place of suffering called Hell.

There are several things about suffering. In the first place

It Is Fire.

F-I-R-E--fire! In Mark, chapter 9, verse 43, we read:

> "And if thy hand offend thee, cut it off: it is better for thee to enter into life maimed, than having two hands to go into hell, into the fire that never shall be quenched."

Suppose you have a hand that is keeping you from Jesus Christ. Suppose you have a hand that is sending your soul to Hell. Suppose your hand has some sin; there is something your hand does you cannot give up, and that thing keeps you from salvation in Jesus Christ. The Bible says "cut it off." Better for you not to have any hands than to go to Hell.

Again in Mark 9, verse 45, it says:

> "And if thy foot offend thee, cut it off: it is better for thee to enter halt into life, than having two feet to be cast into hell, into the fire that never shall be quenched."

If that foot has an enjoyment that you cannot quit; if that foot has a sin it commits that keeps you from God and will send you to Hell, the Bible says "cut it off." Better for you to enter into life without a foot or hand than having feet and hands to be cast into the lake of fire where the worm dieth not and the fire is not quenched.

Verse 47 says:

> "And if thine eye offend thee, pluck it out: it is better for thee to enter into the kingdom of God with one eye, than having two eyes to be cast into hell fire."

If there is something that your eye does that makes you reject Jesus Christ, if there is something your eye does that makes you say no to the Gospel and plunges you toward Hell, the Bible says "gouge it out," "pluck it out." Better for you not to have any eyes or hands and feet than to be cast into the lake of fire where the worm dieth not and the fire is not quenched.

Hell is fire!

I wish people who don't believe the Bible would quit riding under the name of Christianity. I wish people who don't believe what God says in the Bible would quit calling themselves Christians. Oh, my soul hungers for a simple belief in the Word of God.

I wrestled with this thing when I was a kid preacher. Numbers of people tried to counsel with me. Older preachers far down the line tried to tell me I should not preach Hell-fire and brimstone. I had to wrestle about this thing. I went through a brief period where I wondered if there really were fire in Hell. But I had to have a basis; there must be a foundation. There has to be something as the criterion for what you believe. So I decided the Bible is true. I decided this Book is the Word of God, and if this Book says it, I am going to believe it. And this Book is plain about the fires of Hell.

Matthew 25:41 says "everlasting fire." Revelation 20:15 says "the lake of fire," which means liquid fire, lava. Revelation 21:8 says, "The fearful, and unbelieving, and the abominable, and murderers, and whoremongers, and sorcerers, and idolaters, and all liars, shall have their part in the LAKE WHICH BURNETH WITH FIRE AND BRIMSTONE: which is the second death."

In Luke 16:24 the rich man said, "Father Abraham, have mercy on me, and send Lazarus, that he may dip the tip of his finger in water, and cool my tongue; for I am tormented in this flame."

My precious friend, if you have not received Christ as your Saviour, I plead with you, receive Him, come to Him, for in Him alone is escape from the fires of Hell. If you tonight belong to this church, you may be a respectable member, but if you have never been born by the Spirit of God, if you have never been saved, I beg you to come to Christ and be saved. Far better for you to be embarrassed tonight than to be embarrassed when you stand before God.

The second suffering besides fire is

Weeping and Gnashing of Teeth.

In Matthew 22:12, 13 it says about the man who came to the wedding feast having no garment:

> "Then said the king [Jesus] to the servants, Bind him hand and foot, and take him away, and cast him into outer darkness; there shall be weeping and gnashing of teeth."

Falling, burning, weeping, gnashing of teeth! I wish I could describe it--a person gnashing his teeth because of pain.

Recently I got a call from the Chairman of the Board of Deacons at my former pastorate in Garland--one of the best friends I ever had. He said, "Preacher, little Bobby was out in the barn (they live on the farm) playing with some gasoline and the gasoline turned over and little Bobby was just a bundle of fire. He was burned terribly and he has been in the hospital. He will live, but he was burned terribly. Pray for little Bobby."

My heart was broken, crushed! We are so burdened for Bobby; and the folk at Miller Road Church are so heartbroken for Bobby because Bobby has been burned.

Listen, nobody said, "Don't be a fanatic." Oh, they rushed Bobby to the hospital. They got him, smothered the flame, they rushed him to the hospital. Pastor Tom Landers spent all night at the hospital. The deacons gathered around his bed and had prayer because Bobby had been burned. Nobody called them fools; nobody called them fanatics. Nobody said they were narrow-minded because here was a little boy who had been burned. But if these same people plead all night for a sinner to stay out of Hell where they will burn forever, somebody will say they are religious fanatics, fools for Christ.

Not only is there gnashing of teeth and weeping, but there is

Darkness.

Years ago Mrs. Hyles and I were in Colorado for a few days' rest. We went to the Cave of the Winds. This Cave is like Carlsbad Caverns in New Mexico. They took us way back through one tunnel, then we went through a smaller tunnel. All these stalagmites and stovepipes! They were hanging down. One fellow said they were 40 thousand, or 40 million years old--I don't know which. We went through. Water was seeping on our heads. I thought, "Man, oh, don't anybody kick these electric wires! We have been in here thirty-five or forty minutes and if these lights go out, we have had it! Boy, don't anybody kick these electric wires!"

Then all of a sudden it got dark! I looked at my wife--and I didn't look at her! I looked at my hand, and it wasn't there! And I thought, "Dear Lord in Heaven, don't blow a fuse now on these wires!" So dark! So dark you couldn't even see your wife, you couldn't even see your hand--couldn't see a thing, just darkness, total darkness.

And think of it! People who live with you; folks who work with you are headed for eternity without Christ forever, to burn and scream and cry and gnash their teeth in total darkness forever! If you loved them, you would tell them about Jesus. If you cared for them, you would witness to them. We dress in our robes of righteousness, pull our Christianity around us and show off how good we are in a world going to Hell and nobody cares! Our soul in Heaven, when people are headed for outer darkness, without God forever!

Darkness! How many times in the night have I been at the hospital. I can recall in a little town way down near the Louisiana border I received a call at three o'clock in the morning from a little lady who had a one-year-old baby. Our little Becky was a year old then. We stayed all night at the hospital. Little Sheila never pulled out of it completely. Though she still lives, she is afflicted. No one knew what the disease was. I can hear that dear mother as she looked outside and saw the darkness. "Brother Hyles, I wish morning would come! I wish morning would come! Oh, it is not so bad in the daytime, but in the nighttime, at two or at three o'clock in the morning!" I can still hear the cries of that little mother saying, "Brother Hyles, I wish morning would come! I wish morning would come!"

Think of it! In Hell, no morning! No sunshine! No brightness! No glow of God's love! No radiance of the presence of our Saviour! Oh, darkness forever and ever and ever! In a bottomless pit which burneth with fire and brimstone. Darkness! Gnashing of teeth! Suffering! Fire forever!

The suffering of Hell is fire, darkness, weeping and gnashing of teeth, and in the next place the suffering of Hell is

Conscience.

People who know more about the Bible than I do say that when it says in Mark 9:44, "...where their worm dieth not, and the fire is not quenched," their worm means the worm of their conscience. It does not say "the worm," but "their worm." In Mark 9:46 again it says, "Where their worm dieth not, and the fire is not quenched." In Mark 9:48 the third time it says, "Where their worm dieth not, and the fire is not quenched." What worm? The worm of conscience.

Somewhere I heard about a picture entitled "Napoleon in Hell." It pictured the little General Napoleon in Hell. Here was his hell: Around him were gathered all the mothers he had left with dead little babies. Around him were gathered all the little orphaned children caused by his tyranny. Around him were gathered all the widows who were left because of Napoleon's ruthlessness. Napoleon had to look at them, had to look forever in Hell at those orphans, at those widows, at those maimed bodies, and the empty places in the homes. He had to look forever at those because Hell was the conscience of thinking of the awful things he had done on the earth.

My Bible says when people stand before God, the books will be opened, and the deeds done in the body shall be manifest. Oh, the conscience of Hell! I believe there will be songbooks. You will have to hear the songs you heard sung about Jesus, but refused to accept the Gospel. I believe there will be books of sermons that you will have to hear over and over again--sermons you heard but rejected the Gospel after you heard them. Conscience! Oh, the conscience of all the sins, to remind you of all the wickedness, and all the vile, and all the corruption in Hell forever and forever.

We hasten on. Suffering of Hell is fire, darkness, weeping and gnashing of teeth, conscience; but the suffering of Hell also is

Lust.

Revelation 22:11 says:

> "He that is unjust, let him be unjust still: and he which is filthy, let him be filthy still: and he that is righteous, let him be righteous still: and he that is holy, let him be holy still."

So that which is unjust here shall be unjust in eternity. That which is filthy here shall be filthy in eternity. The drunkard here shall be a drunkard in Hell. He will crave liquor in Hell. The lustful here will lust in Hell. The abominable here will be abominable in Hell. There will be no difference except one thing: Brother, when you get to be an alcoholic here, you can find some liquor to satisfy your crave, but in Hell it will be an unsatisfied hunger all the time. Filthy still! No liquor!

How many times have I seen men reach for the bottle in my own presence! I was in a home one time when a man said, "Preacher, I hate to drink in your presence, but I have got to have a bottle." He took that hand, shaking like a leaf in a storm, opened the refrigerator, pulled out the bottle when he could hardly hold it still enough to drink it, and poured it down his mouth, into his stomach, and said, "Preacher, I had to have it!"

But in Hell he will beg and lust for it, but it won't be there. The adulterer will lust, but his lust will not be satisfied. Hell is a place of constant lust. The same unholy passions you had here, you will have there, except there will be no satisfaction offered. Same desires, unholy lusts. He that is filthy shall be filthy still.

Suffering of Hell is fire, darkness, weeping and gnashing of teeth, conscience, lust; and then Hell is a place of

Eternal Death.

Revelation 2:11 speaks about Hell as being the second death. Revelation 20:14 calls Hell the second death. Revelation 21:8 calls Hell the second death. Hell is called eternal dying, eternal death. I believe Hell is that state constantly on that little narrow divide between life and death.

Several years ago I was called into a home at midnight. An eighty-odd-year-old man was dying. I felt his pulse. His hands were cold, his eyes were set in death, it seems. I can hear him as he cried in the night, "Preacher, Preacher, pray for God to let me live! Pray for God to let me live!"

I said, "I will."

Then after awhile he said, "No Preacher, pray for God to let me die."

I can hear the screams of the eighty-year-old man as he said, "O God, let me live! Let me live! Let me live! Let me live!" Then he would scream again and say, "O God, let me die! Let me die! If I can't live, let me die! If I can't die, let me live! But the horror of being here on the borderline! I can see life on one side and death on the other. God, let me go from one to the other!"

The Bible says Hell is eternal dying. People in Hell shall be dying all the time. They will never live. It will be a constant, never-ceasing, endless dying process always, forever and ever.

Sixty people die a minute. Since I have been preaching tonight, over two thousand people have died. March... march...march! Onward! Onward! Two thousand people in the last thirty-five minutes, sixty every minute, thirty-six hundred an hour, eighty-six thousand a day, thirty million people a year! O God, help us! Every time we have a service on Sunday morning in this church, over five thousand people plunge out into eternity, and most of them without God.

How can we sleep at night? Oh, it is a wonder that God doesn't destroy the church of the twentieth century. The churches of our day were built and born in the revival fires of Charles Finney, and Jonathan Edwards, and Dwight Moody, and Billy Sunday. They were born in those revivals. Somebody has said, "Since the days of Billy Sunday, the church of Jesus Christ has made no progress whatsoever." The last shaking this world had was in the days of these fellows who preached Hell-fire and brimstone.

When Jonathan Edwards preached the old sermon, "Sinners in the Hands of an Angry God," people fell under such conviction they reached for the pillars in the church building and held on for fear they would fall that night in the fires of Hell.

Sixty people a minute! Every tick of my watch, another. Tick...Tick...another! Tick...another! Every tick of the watch, every hour of the day, march...march...march--thirty-six hundred people die! Hell, a place of fire! Hell, a place of lust! Hell, a place of conscience! Hell, a place of weeping! Hell, a place of darkness! Hell, a place of eternal separation from all that is good and all that is holy!

But, Thank God, You Don't Have to Go There!

A famous artist painted a picture showing a beautiful forest, a lovely wooded area. But his teacher said, "Never paint a forest without painting a path leading out."

Tonight I have described the doctrine of Hell--the reason,

the location, the prophecy, the duration, the sufferings--all of it; but I am so happy there is a path out. What is the path? Jesus said, "I am the way, the truth, and the life: no man cometh unto the Father, but by me." If you will come to Jesus Christ tonight, you will never have to go to Hell. But if you reject Him, as sure as this Bible is true, without Jesus you will go to Hell. But just as sure as it is true, with Christ you can go to Heaven.

I am so happy tonight that I will never go to Hell. Jack Hyles has taken care of all that already. Thank God, I will never burn one minute in Hell. I will never cry in the darkness of Hell, for Jesus paid it all, all to Him I owe. You say, "Oh, you must be pretty good. If you are not going to Hell, and you know you are going to Heaven, you must be pretty good."

No, I am a scoundrel--just like you. I am no good.

"Oh," you say, "you must live a pretty good life."

The best I can, but I fall short.

But you say, "You know you are going to Heaven; you know you are not going to Hell. You must be spotless, pure."

No, I am not, but I will tell you what. I am trusting Someone who is spotless, pure.

My college president said he was preaching in a revival campaign. He went down to a local restaurant to eat a noon meal. He walked out to pay his bill and he asked the little waitress, "Little Lady, do you know Jesus?"

She looked at him and said, "You are preaching in a revival down at the First Baptist Church, aren't you?"

"Yes, I am."

She said, "Huh! I am not going to go down there because those folks are all hypocrites."

He looked at her and said very tenderly, "But little lady, I didn't come to tell you how wonderful the folks are down there. I came to tell you about Jesus. Can you find anything wrong with Him?"

Great big old tears welled up in her eyes as she looked up

at him and said, "Sir, if more of the people down there would live like Him, more of us people out here would come down there."

I am telling you about Jesus tonight, not the First Baptist Church, not the Baptist denomination. If you will trust Him as Saviour, you will never know what Hell-fire will be for yourself.

Tonight, are you bound for the Promised Land? Or are you afraid if you died tonight, you might go to Hell? If you will come to Jesus, you can settle all that. Bow your heads for prayer, please.

Our Father, we come tonight at the close of this sobering sermon on the subject, "To Hell and Back." Oh, our hearts think of those again and again and again plunging every second into Hell, over and over and over and over again plunging into eternity. Thirty-six hundred an hour, sixty every minute, thirty million people a year, the army continues to march. We pray, O God, that You would help us to be concerned. Help us to care. Help us to witness, and love, and warn, and plead with people not to go to Hell.

While our heads are bowed, our eyes are closed, I can put one hand on the Bible and the other hand high in the air and say, as for me, I will not go to Hell because I know Jesus. I deserve to go to Hell, God knows, but I am not going there because of Jesus. Three cheers for Jesus! Hallelujah for Him who made it possible through His death on the cross. And since I have trusted Him, I am going to Heaven.

How many of you can say, "Brother Hyles, I believe in Hell as much as you do, but, preacher, I'm not going there, for I am in Christ. He is my Saviour and I am His child." Are you willing to lift your hand tonight and say, "I am saved, too, and I am going to Heaven when I die"? As your hand goes up, there ought to be a hallelujah in your heart.

Now dear precious unsaved friends, do you believe the Bible? If you do, you must believe in Hell. How many of you would say tonight, "Preacher, I couldn't raise my hand, couldn't lift it, for I have never trusted Jesus. I do not know that I would go to Heaven if I died, but I wish I did. I believe in Hell, and I don't want to go there"?

8

Russian Roulette

"And as it is appointed unto men once to die, but after this the judgment."--Heb. 9:27.

Russian Roulette is a game played with a pistol and one bullet. A gun is taken, pointed at the head, and the trigger is pulled, knowing not if the bullet is in that particular cylinder. You have one chance in six to die; five in six to live.

It was reported recently in a local newspaper of a young man being killed while playing such a game.

Such folly is unbelievable. Yet, there is a spiritual Russian Roulette played by many that is more dangerous, more tragic, more condemning, and more deadly than any kind of Russian Roulette played with a man-made weapon. There are three dates set in your life. You must face these dates whether you like it or not. You have to face these dates. They could take place any day. They could be today; they could be tomorrow; they could be ten years from now. These dates are indelibly set. In God's wisdom He has set them. We know not when they will be. Yet, if any one of these happened to a lost man today, he would be eternally condemned.

I. THE COMING OF THE LORD JESUS CHRIST MAY BE ANY DAY

"Watch therefore: for ye know not what hour your Lord doth come."--Matt. 24:42.

Now, suppose Jesus came today. Suppose that this moment the clouds of Heaven were to break open and the shout,

"Come forth!" were to come from the lips of the Saviour. Suppose that today the voice of the archangel were to shout and the trump of God were to ring through Heaven's splendor. Suppose the dead in the grave were suddenly to rise and those who were alive and remain, who were saved, should be caught up to meet the Lord in the air. If that took place today, would you be ready?

There is a date set for His coming. The Bible says the angels know not when; the saints in Heaven do not know; even Jesus Christ Himself when on earth said He did not then know. The time is left in the hands of the Father. God the Father has written down on some heavenly note the date of the appearing of the Lord Jesus Christ. It may be October 27, 1976. It may be June 1, 1995. It may be September 11, 1961. I do not know when it will be. You do not know. Jesus on earth did not know. The saints in Heaven do not know. The angels do not know. Angelic hosts do not know. Only God knows.

I ask you a question: Could it be today? It may be out yonder in the year 2000, it may be 1980, it may be in 1975, it may be 1962. But, my friend, there is at least one chance, is there not, that it could be today?

Now, if it could be today, the unsaved are playing spiritual Russian Roulette with the second coming of the Lord Jesus Christ. For there is at least one chance that today might be the last day. There is at least one chance that Jesus might come today. There is at least one chance that you might condemn your soul by saying "No" to Jesus Christ today. It may be June 3, 1987, but it is logical, whenever it is, to be ready for the coming of the Lord Jesus Christ.

I recall when I was a boy, I went to hear an evangelist preach who said that Jesus was coming by Christmas. That was 1936. He said, "Jesus is coming by Christmas." I believed it. I thought He was going to come by Christmas, too. I was scared to death. I went home and cried. I said, "Mother, if He does come by Christmas, what will I do?"

Mother answered, "Son, it all depends on whether you're saved or not."

I got on my knees before Christmas and got converted. I came to Jesus Christ and I know today by my faith in Him and the fact that I have been born again that if Jesus comes today, I will rise to meet Him. If all of a sudden this building were to be made of transcendent splendor and the clouds of Heaven were to open and Jesus Christ the Son of God were to shout and come back in the clouds of glory, I know that I would rise to meet Him in the air.

> **This robe of flesh I'll drop,**
> **and rise**
> **To seize the everlasting prize;**
> **And shout, while passing thro'**
> **the air,**
> **Farewell, farewell, sweet hour**
> **of prayer.**

A date was set for Noah's generation. By Ussher's chronology it was estimated to be May 17, 2448 B. C. Nobody knew when it was. Noah did not know. The people did not know that the day, (possibly May 17, 2448 B. C.) was a date that God had set on His calendar. The people did not know when the destruction would come. Noah did not know the day of the flood. Only God knew. God had placed the date in the heavenly record book of, let us say, May 17, 2448 B. C. When the day came the people tried to get in and tried to get help. Many good people were not prepared. Many people who were sincere were not ready and were destroyed in the flood. Why? Because they played Russian Roulette with the flood.

My precious friend, if I were you today and had not received Christ as my Saviour; if I did not know that if I died today I would go to Heaven; or that if Jesus came today that I would rise to meet Him in the air, I would receive Him now as my Saviour. I would say "Yes" to Christ. I would turn from my sins and turn to Jesus Christ.

I'm trying to say, my precious friends, that Jesus is coming again. I would not play Russian Roulette with my soul and the second coming of Christ. I'm trying to say that the glory of God is going to come from Heaven and Jesus Christ, the Son of God, is coming back again. If you are not saved, if you have not become a Christian, you are playing Russian Roulette with your soul. I beg you, in Jesus' dear name, turn to Christ and be saved by faith in Him and be ready to meet Him when He comes in the air.

Thank God, I settled that myself. I settled that matter a long time ago. You can laugh at it, make fun of it, say what you want to say, get on me for hollering and screaming and shouting and crying and laughing and praising God. Say what you want to say. If you got it the way I got it, you'd have it the way I have it, and you'd act like I act too, a little bit. I'm trying to say this, my dear friend: Receive Jesus before Jesus comes, else you will be left when He comes. Do not play Russian Roulette with the coming of Christ.

Years ago in one of my pastorates a new family moved into our neighborhood and started attending our services regularly. The mother was soon saved and baptized. The children, ages 13, 9, and 6, were saved also and baptized. The father would not receive Jesus. One night the man came to church and heard my sermon on "Hell." As he left he snickered and said, "I'm only 39 years old and I'll get saved in my own time and my own way."

Two days later, on Tuesday morning, a man rushed into the church building screaming, "Come quickly, Pastor! A man is dying." I rushed down the street to find this lost 39-year-old man lifeless on the bed. His wife was over him administering artificial respiration and crying, "He waited too late, Pastor! He waited too late!"

After the doctor pronounced him dead, I was asked to go to the school and tell the children. I gathered the three around me and told them that Daddy was dead. The six-year-old asked, "Where is Daddy now?" What could I say? What a tragedy when men play Russian Roulette with God.

II. DEATH MAY COME ANY DAY

"And as it is appointed unto men once to die..." (Heb. 9:27).

The second date is the date of your death. All men must die. Lamech lived for 777 years, but he died. Enos lived for 905 years, but he died. Caanan lived 910 years, but he died. Seth lived 912 years, but he died. Jared lived 962 years, but he died. Methuselah lived 969 years, but he died.

You, too, must die. God in Heaven has written down on His heavenly records the date that you are going to die. I do not know when it will be. You do not know when. You have no idea what the date will be. God may have written down April 18, 1984. I do not know. But one thing I do know: The Bible says it is appointed unto men once to die and after death the judgment. Every man, every woman, every boy, every girl someday must die, and when you die, you must face God. That means that someday you will stand before God. God will look at you and you will look at Him and you will tell Jesus Himself why you did not receive Him as Saviour.

You're going to die. There's coming a day when they will pronounce you dead. The doctor will look at your family and say, "He's gone," or "She's gone." The family will come and throw themselves over your body and weep, "Don't go! Don't go!" There will be the horrible experience of the funeral service. There will be days of readjustment because you are gone, but you are going to die. I do not know what date it will be, but I do know one thing: it is some day. It may be June 5, 2006. I don't know. It may be March 2, 1986. I don't know. But, it could be today. If there is one chance in a thousand you could die today, that means that if you are not saved you are playing Russian Roulette with your soul. It isn't worth it, my dear friend. The Bible says life is like a shadow that is here and gone; like a flower that blooms in the springtime and fades in the fall; like the dew that comes in the morning and is gone by noontime; like the grass that grows green in the early summer and is brown by the fall and winter.

My father did not know that May 13, 1950, was the date that God had set on His calendar. My father was not a Christian. I preached to my father just before he died. He refused to accept the Lord Jesus Christ. Little did I know when I preached to my father that God had written on His calendar in red letters--May 13, 1950. He didn't know that. I didn't know that. If I had known that, I would have begged him to get saved. If I had known it, I would have gotten on my knees and said, "Dad, don't put it off! You have only a few weeks to live. May 13 is your last day. I beg you, Dad, I beg you, don't put it off." But we didn't know that. However, we did know one thing: it could be May 13, 1950. We knew it could have been the day I talked with him. We did not know and I promised God on the grave of my father that I would preach every Sunday as a dying man to dying people and beg people not to put off this matter of salvation.

Dear friend, someday you are going to die. I'm preaching today to mortal people headed for death and plunging toward eternity, and there is a chance it could be today. I beg you, prepare for death.

I'm happy to say today, not because I'm good, or because I deserve it, or because I do more good things than bad things, but I'm happy to say that if I died, I would be in Heaven. If next Sunday I'm preaching and all of a sudden I slump over and Brother Lyons rushes and catches me and Brother Chamblin says, "He's dying" and deacons rush to give artificial respiration and they carry me out of the building and say, "Brother Hyles is gone; he's dead," don't weep, but rejoice, because I'll be with the Lord Jesus Christ before you get to my body. I know that. I wouldn't trade all the money in the world for that. I wouldn't take anything in this world for the blessed assurance that if I died this minute, I'd be in Heaven with the Lord Jesus Christ.

I've seen folks die in every conceivable place. I've seen them die in the grocery stores. A man who was to speak in our church one night dropped dead before he spoke. I had only met him five minutes before. I do not know when my day is going to be, but it could be today. Today could be the date written on my tombstone. It could be: Jack Hyles--Born 1926; Died--March 15, 1961. It could be that; I don't know. But if I were not ready to meet Christ today and there was one chance in a million that I could die today, I would be playing spiritual Russian Roulette with my soul.

My dear friends, when are some of you folks going to get saved? When are some of you going to walk the aisle to do what you ought to do? There are some folks who say, "I'm going to, I'm going to," yet you are going to wait one of these days and the angry pangs of death are going to come and wrap their ugly tentacles around you and you will be in Hell without God and without hope. I beg you, quit tampering with God's spiritual calendar.

Several years ago I was giving the invitation after a morning sermon. A couple raised their hands for prayer. Neither of them was aware of the other's action. They shook, cried, perspired, and came close to the kingdom. Nevertheless, they rejected the Gospel appeal. After the service they said that they planned to be saved soon. Before a week had passed, she shot him in bloody murder. A short while later, she was killed in a drunken escapade. If they had only known!

A young man recently heard me preach and rejected the Gospel. After the service I talked with him and warned him of the danger of neglect. He laughed and walked away. That night he was killed in a head-on collision on the highway. If he had only known!

Quit playing Russian Roulette with death.

III. YOUR LAST CHANCE FOR SALVATION MAY PASS

"And the Lord said, My spirit shall not always strive with man, for that he also is flesh: yet his days shall be an hundred and twenty years." --Gen. 6:3.

The third date that is set is the date of your last chance of salvation.

There is a time, I know not when,
A place, I know not where,
Which marks the destiny of men
To Heaven or despair.

There is a date on your calendar that marks the last date you will have a chance to get saved. I do not know what it is. Maybe it is April 3, 1965; maybe it's March 25, 1998. I don't know when it is, but it could be May 15, 1961, and this could be the last chance you will ever have at salvation.

The Bible says in Genesis 6:3, "My spirit shall not always strive with man." In Exodus 8:1 it says, "Let Pharaoh alone, he has hardened his heart." In Hosea 4:17 it says, "Ephraim is joined to idols, let him alone." In Genesis 15:16 it says, "The iniquity of the Amorites is not yet full." In Romans 1:26 it says, "God gave them up." In Romans 1:28 it says, "God gave them over."

God someday gets tired of begging you. Soul winners have been in your homes. Some folks have been in your home four, five, six, and seven times. They have begged you to make a stand for God. They have pleaded for you to come to Christ. They have said, "Please don't put it off." One of these days God in Heaven will draw that line and you will step across it and you will have not one more chance as long as you live.

Aaron Burr was a student in Princeton University. Aaron Burr was in a revival meeting back in the days when Princeton was a hotbed for God. They were having an old-fashioned revival and Aaron Burr was under conviction. God spoke to his heart. He walked out one night beneath the stars and looked up to God and said, "God leave me alone! Leave me alone! You leave me alone, God, and I'll leave You alone." God did. From that moment to this God left Aaron Burr alone.

You go right ahead and say "No" to Christ. There is a line drawn and those who continually reject Christ someday will cross that line. Someday you will say "No" the last time and God will say, "I've said 'Please' enough." God will say, "Depart from me into everlasting fire, you workers of iniquity." I beg you, I beg you, don't say "No" to Jesus Christ.

On January 1, 1950, my father sat in my service--about five or six rows back. He was a rough man, a tough-looking man. He used to be a wrestler. I was his preacher boy. On December 31, 1949, I found my father in a tavern. I walked inside that tavern and said, "Dad, you're going home with me this weekend."

Taking my big old Bible that I had preached from for years, I walked up to the bar. The drunks looked at me and wondered what a Bible was doing there. I had never been in a tavern before. I sat down beside my father, put my hand on his shoulder and said, "Dad, you're going to Marshall, Texas, with me today and I'm going to preach to you tomorrow, on January 1, 1950, New Year's Day."

Dad looked at me, shrugged his shoulders and sort of half drunk said, "I'm not going."

I said, "You're going, Dad." (He weighed 235 lbs., was over 6 feet and every inch a man.) I said, "Dad, you weigh almost twice what I weigh, but you're going with me, Dad, if I have to make a scene in this tavern. If I have to drag you bodily, you're going with me."

I took my dad to the car and to Marshall, Texas. On New Year's Eve night we had a Watch Night service, a blessed time. I said to my father, "Dad, are you having a good time?" He looked at me, smiled, and great big tears rolled down his whiskered cheeks, as he said, "Son, they don't have this much fun where I stay."

I took him outside the building and said, "Dad, I'm so happy! I want you to be one of my deacons. I want you to get saved."

Dad began to cry. "Son, I'd love to be one of your deacons."

"Dad, would you receive Christ?"

He didn't receive Christ that night. The next morning I preached to him. He sat about four or five rows back, next to the aisle. An old one-legged deacon, an old country farmer deacon, sat next to him. As I preached, my dad wept. When I got through preaching I just knew he would walk the aisle that day. I gave the invitation; I told everything I knew to tell. I said, "Wouldn't you come to Christ?" He didn't do it.

My old one-legged deacon put his arm around him and my dad reached down and clutched the pew and actually dug his fingernails into the pew as he wept and cried, but didn't come. I closed the service and said, "Tonight he'll come! Tonight he'll come!"

That afternoon we went out in the pasture near the little country church. I put my arm around his big old shoulders and said, "Daddy, I've always wanted you to be a Christian. Dad, I'm a preacher, I'm a pastor; but Dad, you drink, you curse, you are separated from Mother, our home is broken. Wouldn't you receive Christ as your Saviour?"

My dad put his arm on my shoulder (it was almost as big as my body), looked me in the eye and said, "Son, I'm going to do it! I'm going to do it!"

I said, "That's wonderful. That's wonderful. Dad, let's kneel and pray."

"Not now, Son. But I'm going to do it in the spring or early summer. I'm going to Dallas and sell out and I'm going to come to East Texas and buy a little fruitstand or a little grocery store and go into business down here. I'm going to live close enough, Son, to hear you preach every Sunday." Then he said to me for the first time, "Son, I'm proud of you. I want to come back and settle down and I'm going to take you up on that deacon proposition and I'm going to receive Christ and let you baptize me."

That was on January 1, 1950. I lived for the spring and summer. Every time I baptized anyone in that little country baptistry and said, "Buried in the likeness of His death, and raised in the likeness of His resurrection," I pictured myself in the springtime or early summer taking my big old 235-pound dad and lowering him in the water and raising him in newness of life, rejoicing because I had baptized my own dad. I looked forward to the day when I could place my hands on Daddy's head and say, "God bless you, Dad," and have him as a deacon in my church. I longed for it. I lived for it.

On May 13, I had preached a radio sermon at 9 a.m. I finished preaching, went out to the little parsonage in the country and sat down to read the DALLAS MORNING NEWS. The telephone rang. Mrs. Hyles answered. "Rev. Jack Hyles please, long distance calling." I picked up the telephone and a man on the other end of the line said, "This is Mr. Smith. Your dad just dropped dead with a heart attack on the job."

I put my paper down, put my head in my hands and said, "Dear God, it isn't fair! It isn't fair! I've been trying to get folks right with God and my own dad is lost and now has died and as far as I know, was unprepared." I wept and prayed as I went to Dallas, Texas, and followed the hearse down to the little cemetery in Italy, Texas, and watched them put my dad's body in the grave. I went back a few days later and got on my knees on the mound under which my daddy's body rested and said, "Dear Lord, You help me and I'll preach every Sunday just like my dad was in the crowd."

I never go to bed on Saturday night without taking the only picture of my dad that I have, looking at it and saying, "Dear Jesus, tomorrow when I preach I want to preach like Dad was in the service."

Oh, if only I had January 1, 1950, to live over again! I wouldn't let him wait until May or June or the spring or summer. I'd say, "Don't wait, Dad."

We didn't know what the date would be, but God had written back there in the ages of eternity, "May 13, 1950."

> **There is a time, I know not when,**
> **A place, I know not where,**
> **Which marks the destiny of men**
> **To Heaven or despair.**

I beg you, my dear friends, I beg you--Jesus may come today; you may die today; you may cross the line today. I beg you, if you don't know that if you died today you would go to Heaven, receive Him now as your Saviour. Then you can say with me that you know that if you died today, you would go to Heaven.

Don't play Russian Roulette with God.

9

The Great White Throne

"And I saw a great white throne, and him that sat on it, from whose face the earth and the heaven fled away; and there was found no place for them. And I saw the dead, small and great, stand before God; and the books were opened: and another book was opened, which is the book of life: and the dead were judged out of those things which were written in the books, according to their works. And the sea gave up the dead which were in it; and death and hell delivered up the dead which were in them: and they were judged every man according to their works. And death and hell were cast into the lake of fire. This is the second death. And whosoever was not found written in the book of life was cast into the lake of fire."--Rev. 20:11-15.

Herein you find the story of what is known in doctrinal terminology as the Great White Throne Judgment.

In all my ministry I have never thought there was anything as important as keeping folks out of Hell. I have always thought that was the biggest thing. In fact, if I understand the Bible, that is why Jesus left Heaven. That is why He came to earth. That is why He lived on earth for thirty-three years. That is why He went to Calvary. That is why He rose again. That is what He is doing in Heaven tonight, interceding for us, that people might go to Heaven.

That is the biggest thing the church has to do. That is the greatest job of the preacher. That is the most important job of the Christian. Jesus said, "The Son of man is come to seek and to save that which was lost." He said again, "As the Father hath sent me, even so send I you."

Years ago the famous preacher, J. Wilbur Chapman, took a poll of people in his campaigns as to what age they were when they were saved. He found by far the great majority of people who ever came to Christ are saved before they reach the age of twenty. The greatest majority of people are saved between the ages of twelve and sixteen. For example, how many of you here received Christ somewhere between ten and fifteen? Well, you can see the huge response of those who are here, saved between the ages of ten and fifteen.

He took also a poll and found that when a man passes 25 years of age--man or woman--he has one chance in 1,000 to get saved. Only one person in 1,000 is saved after he is 25. If a person passes 35, he has one chance in 50,000 to be saved. If a person passes 45 without Jesus Christ, he has one chance in 200,000 to get saved. If a man passes 55 without Christ, he has one chance in 300,000 to get saved. And if a man passes 75 without Jesus, he has one chance in 700,000 to be saved, or one chance in almost a million.

Now you can see why it is tremendously important that we stay after sinners, that we try to get folks saved. And so constantly we are after people, trying to get them to receive the Lord Jesus Christ.

Now a word about the background. We are looking tonight for the rapture of the church. That is the event when the Lord Jesus Christ will come, the trumpet of God shall sound, the dead in Christ shall be raised, those who are alive and remain shall be caught up to meet the Lord in the air, and for seven years we will be with Him in the air.

While that seven years transpires in the air, on the earth will be what is known as the Great Tribulation period, the time of suffering, of war, of famine, of death, of bloodshed. On the earth, a seven-year period known as the

Great Tribulation period. In Heaven, the judgment seat, the marriage of the Lamb. We will be there seven years. The earth, in the Tribulation for seven years.

At the end of that time we will come back with Jesus to establish a kingdom on the earth. For one thousand years, we as God's children, shall rule and reign with the Lord Jesus Christ here upon this earth. We shall be priests of God and shall rule and reign with Christ for a thousand years.

Now at the end of that thousand years will take place what is known as the Great White Throne Judgment. Have you ever heard anybody pray thusly, "Dear Lord, help me to live so as some day I may appear before the Great White Throne"? Now I don't want to pray like that. I don't intend to appear before the Great White Throne, for the Great White Throne Judgment is the closing judgment of the unsaved dead.

Now tonight for our message I will use the word "seconds" and show you a series of second things that will summarize the study of the Great White Throne Judgment found in Revelation, chapter 20, verses 11 through 15.

In the first place, I call your attention to the second resurrection. In the second place, I call your attention to the second judgment. In the third place, I would speak on the second Adam. In the fourth place, the second death. In the fifth place, the second birth.

Now look if you will in the first place to

The Second Resurrection.

Turn to Revelation 20:5:

> "But the rest of the dead lived not again until the thousand years were finished. This is the first resurrection."

In verse 5 we find the resurrection of the saved, when those of us who are saved shall be caught up to meet the

Lord Jesus Christ in the air. I remind you of this: All the people will not be raised at the same time. I hear people talk about, "At the last day," "the resurrection." There will not be any such thing as the resurrection, one general resurrection. The Bible says when Jesus comes, two shall be grinding at the mill. One shall be taken; the other left. Two shall be in bed. One shall be taken; the other left. And so at the first resurrection, which takes place at the rapture of the church, only Christians will be resurrected. For our message tonight we speak of the second resurrection.

Now, after the Christians are gone, the Bible says the unsaved will be left. Those who die in their sins will be still in the grave. And it says, "They lived not again until the thousand years were finished."

Just suppose tonight, here is a man who is saved; here is a wife who is lost. They die, they are buried. Now that man, that saved person, will be raised from the dead when Jesus comes for His own. When the trumpet of God sounds and the dead in Christ rise, the dead in Christ will be raised when Jesus comes for His own. But this lost wife over here in the grave, right beside the saved person, won't rise at the second coming of Christ. The lost person will not rise when Jesus comes for His own, but will stay in the grave a thousand and seven years longer than the saved. The saved rise before the millennium; the lost rise after the millennium. There are two different resurrections.

Look at verses 12 and 13:

> "And I saw the dead, small and great, stand before God; and the books were opened: and another book was opened, which is the book of life: and the dead were judged out of those things which were written in the books, according to their works. And the sea gave up the dead which were in it; and death and hell delivered up the

dead which were in them: and they were judged every man according to their works."

Now there is going to be a second resurrection. At the second resurrection, at the end of the thousand-year reign of Christ upon the earth, the unsaved dead will be raised--the drunkards, the harlots, the whoremongers, the liars, the thieves, the sorcerers, the adulterers, the idolaters--all unbelievers; those who rejected the Gospel of Christ, those who, in services like this, said no to Jesus Christ; those who believed they knew more than God--the infidels, the liberals, the modernists--all the people who laughed at the Bible and thought they were too smart for the Word of God, they will be raised at the second resurrection.

Now notice the words "death" and "hell." It says that death and Hell will deliver up the dead which were in them. At death a lost man's body goes to the grave, but his soul goes to Hades. Actually the word "hell" in verse 23 is translated from "hades." Hades is the place where the rich man is in Luke, chapter 16, when he lifted up his eyes, being in torments and said, "Father Abraham, send Lazarus, that he may dip the tip of his finger in water, and cool my tongue; for I am tormented in this flame." His body was in the grave; his soul was in Hades.

At the second resurrection, the soul of that rich man, and the soul of everybody will come from Hades, their bodies will come from the graves, and the soul and body shall be reunited, and both body and soul shall be cast in the final lake of fire.

Let me say again--you will hear me say it a thousand times in this pulpit--I believe in a burning, literal Hell of fire. If the Bible is not true on Hell, we have no reason to believe the Bible is true on anything else either. If it is not fire in Hell as Jesus said in the Bible, we can say salvation does not mean exactly what it says. Heaven is not real, if we do not believe the Scriptures on Hell. Jesus said Hell was fire. We modern folks, we have gotten too educated. We are too scientific. I don't care what you believe, my friends; the Bible is true. The Bible says, "Let God be true and every man a liar." And so the souls of people who die in their sins are in Hell, in conscious torment tonight.

But at the end of the millennium, the souls shall come from Hades, the body shall come from the grave, the body and the soul of the unsaved shall be reunited, and Jesus Christ Himself shall take both body and soul and cast them into the lake of fire.

My precious friend, if you are hoping in some way, that maybe you will go to purgatory and somebody will pull you out of purgatory, you have got your eggs in the wrong basket. My Bible says there is a place called Heaven, there is a place called Hell, and between the two there is a great gulf fixed, and no one can pass from one to the other. When you die, you have sealed your destiny. They can call prayer meetings and pray for your departed spirit; they can call a High Mass or a Low Mass, but if you have not received Christ, you are lost forever in the pit of an eternal Hell.

So the body of the unredeemed will come from the grave; the soul from Hades. Jesus will later cast both body and soul back into Hell.

Now we have seen the second resurrection. We hasten on to what is known as

The Second Judgment.

Now the second judgment takes place after the second resurrection. Look in verse 13 again:

> "And the sea gave up the dead which were in it; and death and hades delivered up the dead which were in them [that is the second resurrection]: and they were judged every man according to their works [that is the second judgment]."

We have preached to you before about the judgment seat of Christ. I told you about a time that is coming when all believers shall receive their rewards. And not a single lost person will be at that judgment. If you do not remember a thing I say, do not forget this: There will never in this world, there will never in the world to come, be a time when all the people, saved and unsaved, will be brought before the same judgment of God. There will not be any such time. Our sins were judged in Jesus on the cross of Calvary. That takes care of that. He judged my sins for me. I will never stand before God as far as salvation is concerned. I must stand before God when all Christians stand before Him. Before the millennium, before the thousand years, we must stand before Him to get our rewards. At the end of the thousand years, will be the second judgment, and that will be the judgment of the unsaved. The unsaved will be at the second judgment.

Before the second judgment, verse 11 says, "And I saw a great white throne, and him that sat on it, from whose face the earth and the heaven fled away...." Did you see that? At the Great White Throne Judgment, when all the redeemed are resurrected and stand before God, then the Bible says, "the earth and the heaven shall flee away."

There is going to be a day when the earth shall flee away. In II Peter it says it shall melt with fervent heat. There is going to be a day when even Heaven itself shall flee away. In the Sermon on the Mount in Matthew, Jesus said that Heaven shall pass away, earth shall pass away, but the Word of God abideth forever. And so before the Great White Throne Judgment, Heaven shall pass away, and the earth shall pass away.

Now why shall the earth pass away? Because God will not have anything contaminated by sin, and this earth has been contaminated by sin. And so God is going to give us a new earth and a new heaven, the starry heaven. And when this time comes, somewhere in the skies, in the third Heaven maybe, when Jesus Christ, the Son of God, sits on the Great White Throne and all the unredeemed stand before Him, Heaven shall flee away, earth shall flee away, and then shall be a new heaven and a new earth.

May I say again: This judgment in Revelation 20 is not for the saved; it is only for the unsaved. Not a single saved person will stand before this judgment. Dear friend, rest at ease. If you are saved, you are not going to stand before God. I have heard folks say, "Well, I hope I get saved in the end." Brother, if you don't get saved in the beginning, you won't get saved in the end. If you don't get saved now, you won't get saved at all. There is not going to be a time when God is going to take us and decide then whether we go to Heaven or Hell. That was decided the moment you received Christ as your Saviour.

These people this morning who came down these aisles and by faith received Jesus Christ as their Saviour, that once and for all settles their going to Heaven. Why? Because when they accepted Him, they immediately got a release from this Great White Throne Judgment of God. Only the unsaved will be there.

And this Great White Throne Judgment of God is not a judgment of salvation, but a judgment for degrees of punishment. Some are going to burn hotter than others. (That is not a very good way to put it, is it? But that is about the way it is.) But some will receive more punishment than others. Just as some at the judgment seat shall receive more rewards than others; at the Great White Throne Judgment some shall receive more punishment than others. Let me say this, too: Those who reject Jesus Christ the most, those who say no to the Gospel, shall burn in Hell far more uncomfortable than those who do not.

Here is a good man who hears the Gospel one time. He lived where there was no gospel preaching. Only one time did he ever hear the Gospel. He is a good husband, a good father, but he rejected the Gospel of Christ. Yes, he will go to Hell because he received not the Saviour. But he will not burn as much as this fellow who heard the Gospel every Sunday. Some of you folks who belong to a church but have never been born again--you go to church every Sunday and you are reminded every Sunday, "If you die, would you go to Heaven? Do you know if you died tonight, you would go to Heaven?" Again, and again, and again, and again the preacher said that and your conscience is pricked. You know you are not saved. You know you have not been born again. You know you are lost. The Bible says those people who have received much shall be punished more. And people who have heard the Gospel much and rejected many, many times the story of Christ, those who have lived in awful sin, shall get more punishment than those who have not heard it so often.

And so the White Throne Judgment is not for salvation, but for degrees of punishment.

Let's picture it here. Here is the great throne over here. On the throne is the Lord Jesus Christ. Ken, can you and John imagine you are lost, for a minute? I will have you both stand before the throne. Ken is standing before the throne. He has been a bootlegger, he has beaten his wife (you didn't know all that about Ken, did you?), he is a first-class crook. He has come to church all his life but never believed the Gospel of Christ. He does not believe the Bible is the Word of God. He does not believe that Jesus Christ is God's Son. He snickered and laughed at his wife. She carried the children to church all her life while Ken laughed, mocked, and made fun of the old-time religion and the Bible being the Word of God and Jesus being the Son of God. When he stands before God, he will suffer more hell than will somebody else who didn't have the opportunities that he had.

Here is John. He is a good man. He drinks soda. That is the very strongest drink John drinks. John stands before God.

God says, "John, have you ever heard the Gospel?"

"Yes, I heard it one time. When I was a little boy, I heard the Gospel."

"Did you receive it?"

"No I didn't."

"John, have you been a good husband?"

"Yes."

"Have you been a good father?"

"Yes."

"Have you been a good citizen?"

"That's right."

"Have you lived a pretty clean life?"

"That's right."

"John, you will still have to go to Hell, but yours will be say 190° Fahrenheit and yours, Ken, will be 640° Fahrenheit!"

Don't you tell me that the drunkard in the gutter who beat his wife and drank up the food from the little children, and made them orphans and made a wreck out of his wife and children, and said no to the Gospel and made light of the Word of God, will not suffer more than one little child fifteen years old, perhaps, who died but rejected the Gospel of the Lord Jesus Christ. I don't believe it. It says that they shall be judged every man according to his works.

So we have the second resurrection. That is, when the unsaved are raised from the dead. We have the second judgment. That is, when the unsaved stand before God.

Now in the third place, we come to what is known as

The Second Adam.

In I Corinthians, chapter 15 and verse 22 it is mentioned. Jesus Christ is called the second Adam. In the first Adam, all died. In the second Adam, all became alive. Whereas through the first Adam, sin came into the world; through the second Adam, righteousness came into the world. So Jesus is called the second Adam.

Who is going to judge? In verse 11 of Revelation 20:

> "And I saw a great white throne, and him that sat on it, from whose face the earth and the heaven fled away; and there was found no place for them."

In John, chapter 5, the Bible says all judgment is given to Jesus Christ. The second Adam is going to sit on the throne.

May I say this: In that day Jesus Christ will not be the loving, tender Saviour wanting to save. Tonight He is. Tonight Jesus says, "Him that cometh to me, I will in no wise cast out." In that day He will not give you a chance to come to Him. For Jesus, the Son of God, the one you rejected, the one who tried to save you, the one who died for you, sits on the throne and He calls your name. Here is Jesus, and here is the unsaved person. For the first time in his life he has to stand face to face with Jesus Christ and give an account for why he rejected the Gospel. Here is the unsaved one standing before Jesus. Too late to get saved at all, you will have to get saved now, for it will be too late then.

It is said a judge in a large city was walking along the walk near some water one day. He saw a young man drowning. He rushed to his rescue, took off his coat, jumped in the water, and brought the man to safety. He saved his life. The man, so grateful, expressed his gratitude to the judge. The judge literally had saved him from death.

A few months passed, and this same young man committed some crime against society and was brought before this same judge. The judge sentenced him to whatever the penalty was.

The man said, "But say, Judge, you remember me, don't you?"

Sternly the judge answered, "Sir, I don't recall."

He said, "Judge, remember a few months ago you were walking near the water and I was drowning? You pulled off your coat, jumped in the water and pulled me to safety? You saved my life, Judge. Now I know you won't want to send me to jail."

The judge looked at him and said, "Young man, that day I was your saviour; today I am your judge."

Jesus Christ is your Saviour tonight. He wants to save you. He will save any child, any man, any woman who will come by faith to Himself. He will save you. He will forgive your sins. He will make you a home in Heaven. He will save you from the fires of Hell. He will make you His child. All that belongs to Him shall belong to you. And you can leave this building tonight saying, "I know that I know that I know I am a child of God." But in that day the loving Saviour will be your Judge.

But you say, "Dear Lord, I am the one who is on the prospect file down at the First Baptist Church in Hammond. They always beg me. I thought about coming when I got around to it."

"I was your Saviour then; now I am your Judge," He will say.

Jesus, the second Adam, shall be the judge.

We have seen the second resurrection; we have seen the second judgment; we have seen the second Adam; now may I remind you of

The Second Death.

Look at verse 14:

> "And death and hades were cast into the lake of fire. This is the second death."

The second resurrection shall take place first. After the second resurrection, the unsaved will be judged at the second judgment. They will be judged by the second Adam, and then they will suffer the second death. Here it is. They call the names...

John Peabody!

Mary Smith!
Jack Johnson!
Joe Jones!

They call the names! They stand before God, and God opens the books. The books are opened, and another book which is the Book of Life, and Revelation 20:15 says those not found written in the Book of Life were cast into the lake of fire. This is the second death.

Do you know what America needs? A generation of Hell-fire-and-brimstone preachers. Listen to me tonight. Every religious revival this world has ever known, every spiritual revival, has been built on preaching the judgment and the wrath and the fury of a righteous and holy and just God. I am not discounting God's love. I believe in preaching about the love of God. But as Billy Sunday used to say, "You can't love flowers unless you hate weeds." You can't love God unless you hate sin. For it was sin that nailed the Saviour to the cross. And the more you love Him, the more you appreciate Him, the more you hate that which caused Him to suffer on the cross of Calvary.

Billy Sunday, Dwight Moody, R. A. Torrey, Paul Rader, Gypsy Smith, George Truett--oh, how many more names we could recall; men of yesterday--Savonarola, Martin Luther, John Wesley, John Calvin, John Huss--were every one men who realized our God is a consuming fire. My precious friend, you hear me tonight! You someday will stand before God and if you are not saved, you will stand before Him and God shall say, "Cast him into outer darkness. Bind him hand and foot, for he has not received the invitation to come to my supper."

The second death. In chapter 21, verse 8 it says the same thing:

> "But the fearful, and unbelieving, and the abominable, and murderers, and whoremongers, and sorcerers, and idolators, and all liars,

> shall have their part in the lake which burneth with fire and brimstone: which is the second death."

Nowadays theology says, "Don't tell folks about Hell. Don't tell them they are going to Hell if they die and are lost. Tell them that in Jesus they have the more abundant life."

That is right. You do have the more abundant life. But brother, lost people are going to have an abundant death, and you had better tell them about that, too. I believe Jesus does give abundant life. Thank God, I have been happy ever since I came to Christ. Now I am happy in the Lord. I love the prayer life, the Bible study, and the fellowship with God. But there is one thing I do know: The same God who accepts sinners also condemns them to Hell if they receive not the Gospel of Christ.

The second death; the fires of Hell. Some of you folks will say, "Well, I just don't believe Hell is real fire." Well, you have a right not to believe it, but you can't say you believe the Bible and not believe Hell is real fire.

And you have a right to believe what you want to believe, but don't you call yourself a Christian. Don't you call yourself a Bible-believer. Don't call yourself a fundamental believer in the Gospel of Christ if you don't believe what Jesus said about Hell being fire. Jesus said, "Then shall he say also unto them on the left hand, Depart from me, ye cursed, into everlasting fire...."

But you say, "He didn't mean fire." He may not have meant fire, but He said fire, didn't He? And as the little girl said, "Mamma, if Jesus didn't mean what He said, why didn't He say what He means?"

He said fire. Again He said in Mark 9:44, "Where their worm dieth not, and the fire is not quenched." Over and over and over again we are reminded in the Bible that those who reject the Gospel of Christ must suffer the second death.

My friends in the balcony, on the lower floor, up here--I beg you tonight, if you have never by faith received Jesus Christ, flee to the Son of God who alone can save you from the fires of Hell.

After the Great White Throne Judgment will come the second resurrection. After the second resurrection will come the second judgment. On the throne shall be the second Adam, and there shall be a second death.

But you say, "Preacher, how can I escape the second resurrection? How can I escape the second judgment? How can I escape facing, at the awful time, the second Adam? How can I escape the fires of the second death?"

I am glad you asked me. That is by being participants in the second birth.

The Second Birth

The Lord Jesus said, "Ye must be born again." Anybody who has the second birth will not have to suffer the second death. If you have not received the second birth, you have to suffer the second death. Jesus stands, the books are opened, another book is opened, the Book of Life. You stand before God. God looks at you.

Jesus Christ says, "Is your name in the book?"

You say, "Dear Lord, it must be. I was a good church member."

He says, "Is your name in the book?"

"Well," you say, "I guess so. I was baptized."

"But is your name in the book?"

"Well," you say, "I imagine it is. I had an attendance pin. I didn't miss for fourteen years in Sunday School."

"But is your name in the book?"

"Well, I think so. I gave to the Community Chest every year. I have a little sticker on the window."

"But is your name in the book?"

"Well, I think so. I was a good husband."

"Is your name in the book?"

"Well, I guess so. I was a good father."

"Is your name in the book?"

"Well, I paid my debts."

"IS YOUR NAME IN THE BOOK?"

There is only one thing: Have you been born again? If you have, you will go to Heaven. If you haven't, you are going to Hell regardless of all the good things you have done. Only one determining question: Have you been born again? If you have been born again, thank God, you will miss all of this. If you haven't been born again, you will stand before God as the books are opened.

In Philadelphia, Pennsylvania, Ethan Allen stood up to testify at a Christian meeting. Ethan Allen was for years an officer in the United States Army. Allen gave this testimony at a Businessmen's luncheon:

> "I married the girl of my dreams. We were so in love, so happy. But she was a Christian; I was an infidel. I watched her go to church Sunday after Sunday. I looked at her life, listened to her prayers. I saw her Bible stained with tears. I was an infidel. I laughed at her as she walked off to church, made fun of her as she prayed. I thought she was foolish for reading the Word of God. I was an infidel."

Ethan Allen said:

> "After awhile, gentlemen, God gave us a baby, a precious little girl. Oh, we loved her! How we loved her! When she was an infant, her mother carried her to Sunday School every Sunday. When she was a Beginner--four, five, six--every Sunday she was at church. Every Sunday night--back to the Sunday night service. Every

Wednesday night--to mid-week prayer service. She never missed. Every week she went with her mother."

Then said Ethan Allen:

"When she was six--to church with Mother. Seven--to church with Mother. Eight, nine, ten, eleven--to church with Mother. But when she got to be about twelve, I began taking her with me to night clubs, to dance halls, to high balls. She had a good time.

"Finally she began to tell her mother, 'Mother, I don't want to go to church today. I am too sleepy. Daddy and I stayed out so late last night.'"

Ethan Allen continued:

"I would laugh under my breath and say, she is not going to follow the old-time religion of her mother. I am so happy about that. Her mother would plead and beg, 'Honey, please go with Mother. Please go with Mother.' But I would say, 'Honey, you stay home if you want to.' So she would say no to her mother.

"Finally on Sunday nights I would take her out to the dance halls or some night club with me, and we would have a big time painting the town red while Mother was at the church house weeping her eyes out because her daughter had gone into sin."

He said:

"Finally our daughter quit going to church. She

never went with her mother. She was a beautiful girl, fifteen or sixteen years of age. We loved her dearly. Her mother was a Christian; I an infidel. She was following Daddy's footsteps.

"But one night she was out with a gang of kids in a carriage. They had been swimming, and she caught cold. After awhile it went into pneumonia. In those days we didn't have penicillin and all the other cures we have now. So before long she was at the point of death.

"The doctor called me in and said, 'Mr. Allen, your girl is dying.'"

Allen looked at those businessmen and said:

"I went in and looked at my little girl--just a teen-ager. Her mother had served Jesus Christ; I was an infidel. I looked at her and my daughter said to me, 'Daddy, I am dying, am I not?'

"I replied, 'Yes, Honey. You are going to die.' Then I began to weep. Her mother was crying. But there was not a tear in our little girl's eyes. She said, 'Daddy, I want to know one thing. All my life Mother has gone one way, and you have gone the other way. Now Daddy, since I am dying, I have got to know the answer. I have got to know. I love you, Daddy. I love you and I trust you and believe what you say. Daddy, while I am dying, should I die Mommy's way or your way?'"

Ethan Allen said:

"I began to cry. Then I threw my body on hers and said, 'Honey, choose Mother's way! Choose Mommy's way! Quickly, honey! Choose Mommy's way!'"

Ethan Allen said:

> "Before I could get it said, she had gone off to meet the Lord Jesus. I will never know until I face God whether or not she chose Mommy's way or Daddy's way!"

Oh, in Jesus Christ tonight is escape from judgment. There is salvation forever. Heaven with Christ and the saints. That is the best way. Choose Mommy's way!

Oh, Thomas Paine thought he could live without God. When Paine came to die he said, "I wish I had never lived!"

Voltaire laughed and mocked at God, and when Voltaire came to face death, he said, "O Jesus Christ, O Jesus Christ! It is hell to be left alone!"

Thomas Hobbs wrote book after book denying the efficacy of the Gospel of Christ. And when Thomas Hobbs came to die, he said, "I am taking a fearful leap into the dark! O Christ! O Jesus!"

My precious friends, in Christ tonight, in the second birth, you can know the second Adam; you can escape the second death, the second resurrection, and the second judgment, if you know Christ in the second birth.

Do you know Him tonight? Will you be at the first resurrection, or at the second? Will you be at the first judgment, or the second? Will you suffer the second birth, or the second death? Do you know what it is to receive Christ by faith and know that your sins are forgiven? If you don't, you can, just as easy as a lifted prayer to God, saying, "God, be merciful to me, a sinner." I recommend Him to you tonight. Oh, how wonderful! Oh, how marvelous is our Saviour's love for me!

I stand amazed in the presence
Of Jesus the Nazarene,
And wonder how He could love me,
A sinner, condemned, unclean.

He loves you tonight. He will save you. Do you know that if you die, you will go to Heaven? Are you sure you are saved? Have you been born again? Have you had the experience of the second birth? If you have, don't worry about the second resurrection. Don't worry about the second judgment. Don't worry about the second death, because you have the second Adam in your heart by experiencing the second birth.

Will you bow your heads for prayer?

PRAYER:

Our Father, we come tonight in this sober thought, realizing some day the unsaved must stand before God. Some day those who have not received the Saviour must face Him. Oh, what an awful day! When the books are opened, and death and Hades deliver up their dead, and the people who are unsaved shall be judged according to their works and cast into the lake of fire! We thank Thee, our Saviour, that we have received Christ. We thank Thee for refuge in Him.

Our heads are bowed, our eyes are closed. I have mentioned this, but a famous artist was teaching one of his pupils. The pupil painted a beautiful scene, a beautiful forest scene. The trees were lovely, the forest was beautiful. The master came and looked at the picture. The young man was so proud, so happy. The master, as he observed the picture, made this criticism, "Young man, never paint a forest without a path leading out."

I think I can say that to every preacher: Never preach about Hell, never preach about the judgment, without a path leading out.

Thank God, there is a path! That path is Jesus who said, "I am the way, the truth, and the life."

Do you know Him tonight? Have you trusted Him? Is He your Saviour?

Can you say, "Brother Preacher, I have received Him as Saviour. He is mine; I am His. I don't worry about the second judgment for I won't be there. I don't worry about the second resurrection. That won't affect me, for I have received the second Adam and experienced the second birth. I know I have. I belong to Christ. He is my Saviour, and I know it"? Will you lift your hands up high?

As you drop your hands, keep your heads bowed. How many of you will say, "Brother Preacher, I could not lift my hand tonight. I do not know that I am saved. I have not been born again. I am not a child of God. I wish I were. I don't want to go to Hell. I want to go to Heaven. I want to be saved. But I will have to confess tonight I do not know that I am a Christian. I wish you would pray for me. I want to know it. I don't want to go to Hell, I want to be saved some day. Preacher, pray for me"?

I wonder how many of you will lift your hand tonight, and by the uplifted hand you will be saying, "Include me in your prayer." Lift it now and I will pray for you.

10

Words of Jesus

Tomorrow our new little baby will be home from the hospital and so I have an idea I will be scalding bottles and hanging out diapers, etc. But the first task I always have the first day any baby of ours comes home from the hospital is, to tell them salvation's plan from Adam in the Garden of Eden, until Jesus comes in the clouds of glory. So Cindy has a dry, dull day ahead of her tomorrow because she will hear Daddy tell her that Adam brought sin into the world!

When our first child, Becky, who was eight years old yesterday, came home, I told her how Jesus loved her, that she was born in sin, that when she got old enough to know right from wrong she would be accountable for her sins, and that if she would repent of her sins and put her trust and faith in the finished work of the cross of Calvary, for Jesus died for her, she could be saved.

To each of our children I have told that story the first day home from the hospital. I haven't won any of them to Christ yet on that particular day! They have been hard cases! It has taken a little while to break through the crust, but I have told them that immediately. And through these years I have always believed that there is an unusual power in the Word of God even to boys and girls.

I say today that I believe this Bible has more power than it has ever had. Jesus said in Mark 13, verse 31, "Heaven and earth shall pass away: but my words shall not pass away."

I am speaking this morning on the subject, "The Words of Jesus." I have spoken before about His blood, about His name, about His hands, about His life; and now today, "The Words of Jesus."

Through the years many people have been helped by His words. How many people at a funeral service have been strengthened as the preacher quoted Jesus when He said:

> "Let not your heart be troubled: ye believe in God, believe also in me. In my Father's house are many mansions: if it were not so, I would have told you. I go to prepare a place for you. And if I go and prepare a place for you, I will come again, and receive you unto myself; that where I am there ye may be also."--John 14:1-3.

Or, how many people at times of heartbreak have heard the Saviour say:

> "I will not leave you comfortless: I will come to you...And I will pray the Father, and he shall give you another Comforter, that he may abide with you for ever; Even the Spirit of truth...."
> --John 14:18, 16, 17.

Or, how many people have found comfort and salvation at the altar or in a great revival campaign, or in a Sunday morning service like this with the words of Jesus:

> "For God so loved the world, that he gave his only begotten Son, that whosoever believeth in him should not perish, but have everlasting life."--John 3:16.

Or, how many people have found salvation at Jesus' words in John 6:37--

> "All that the Father giveth me shall come to me; and him that cometh to me I will in no wise cast out."

Or, how many people have found salvation at the words of Jesus when He said:

> "He that believeth on him is not condemned: but he that believeth not is condemned already ...."--John 3:18.

Or, how many folks have received salvation at the words of Jesus when He said:

> "He that believeth on the Son hath everlasting life: and he that believeth not the Son shall not see life; but the wrath of God abideth on him." --John 3:36.

Or, how many people have been comforted in times of tears when they heard the words of Jesus:

> "Come unto me, all ye that labour and are heavy laden, and I will give you rest."--Matt. 11:28.

Or, how many people who were hungry have been comforted to hear Jesus say, "I am the bread of life."

Or, how many thirsty people have been comforted when Jesus said, "I am the living water."

Or, how many people who have lost loved ones have been comforted to hear Jesus say, "I am the resurrection and the life."

Or, how many people who have been beside those who were ill and seen them pass away, have been comforted to hear Jesus say, "I am the way, the truth, and the life."

Or, those who are wandering have heard Him say, "I am the good shepherd."

Or, those who are groping in darkness have heard Him say, "I am the door."

Or, those who are yearning for truth have heard Him say, "I am the truth."

Or, those who have lost themselves have heard Him say, "I am the way."

Or, those who have had their own deathbeds have heard Him say, "I am the life."

Again, and again, and again we have been strengthened and built up and even saved by the wonderful words of our blessed Saviour.

Now I want you to notice with me this morning

His First Words.

First words are tremendously important. For example, at the hospital the other day I looked at my little Cindy through the window and she smiled. I could hear her say just as plain as day, "Daddy!" Why, anybody would know what she was saying! It was obvious! Now you don't believe that. Maybe she didn't say it. But anyway, it seemed to me she was saying that!

Anyway, we love to grasp for first words. What did they say first? You recall the day that little child said "Daddy" for the first time. What the child really said was "Bla Du Glub Goo!" And you said, "That's Daddy, isn't it? Why, it is so plain, anybody can see it!" And so first words are tremendously important.

The same was true with the Lord Jesus Christ. What were Jesus' first words in the Bible? In Mark, the first thing Jesus is recorded to have said is, "Repent ye, and believe the gospel." He started talking about the Gospel immediately. Now when He said, "Repent ye, and believe the gospel," would you not think it tremendously important to heed the words spoken by Jesus?

His first words recorded in Matthew were when John came and Jesus said, "Baptize me, John." And John said, "Not so, dear Lord. I am not worthy to baptize you. I am not worthy to even unloose the shoes on your feet." But

Jesus said, "Now suffer it to be fulfilled, John. To fulfill all righteousness I must indeed be baptized."

So could we not say, if the first words that Jesus Christ said in Mark were of the Gospel, the Gospel is important? Could we not say, if the first words which Jesus spoke in Matthew were concerning baptism, that baptism is important?

Then we go down to Luke. The first words Jesus said as recorded in Luke were when He was about twelve years old in the Temple; "I must be about my Father's business." What is the Father's business? Jesus tells us in Luke 19:10, "I came to seek and to save that which was lost."

The first words of Jesus recorded in the book of John were spoken to sinners, "What seek ye?" The first word in Matthew was spoken about baptism. The first word in Mark was spoken about the Gospel. And the first words in Luke were spoken about winning sinners to the Lord Jesus Christ. And so I would say that salvation is important. Jesus started His ministry speaking about salvation. I would say baptism is important. Jesus started His ministry speaking about baptism. I would say that being about the Father's business is important, because Jesus started His ministry speaking about being about the Father's business. Those are the first words of the Saviour.

Now I call your attention not only to the first words of Jesus, but to

The Last Words of Jesus.

The last recorded words in Matthew and Mark are the words of the Great Commission:

> "Go ye therefore, and teach all nations, baptizing them in the name of the Father, and of the Son, and of the Holy Ghost: Teaching them to observe all things whatsoever I have commanded you: and, lo, I am with you alway, even unto the end of the world."--Matt. 28:19, 20.

Last words are tremendously important. You treasure beyond value the last words of loved ones who pass away.

The last words I ever heard my father say on this earth were, "Son, I will see you in the spring." And you have treasured up in your little white sanctuaries down in the holy of holies of your heart, many, many wonderful memories of the last words of those whom you loved as dear as life itself.

How much grace and strength God gave Mr. Roberts when our dear Mrs. Roberts passed away last week. We went to his home a few minutes after his wife had gone to Heaven, and we discussed the death with him. He opened his Bible, and I could see the stain of tears on the Bible. There were Scriptures underlined, and he said, "I want to show you some Scriptures where I found comfort and strength." And he said, "You know what we did just a while ago? Just before she passed away at ten o'clock, we had breakfast and bowed and prayed together." Isn't that wonderful? And I am sure he will treasure those words his wife said just before she went to Heaven.

If those words were important, then the last words Jesus gives are important. Let's hover up close. Let's hear what He said. Dear Jesus, what is the one thing You want to tell us? What is the one apex, the one pinnacle thing You want us to know of all the things You have said? You have raised the dead; You have healed the sick; You have cast out devils; You have caused blind people to see; You have caused the deaf to hear, the dumb to speak, the dead to live, the sick to be well. And now, dear Jesus, of all of these things, what would You say was the most important thing of all?

Jesus says in His last words in Matthew and Mark, "Go and preach the Gospel to every creature."

Somebody says, "Why does Brother Hyles always try to get sinners saved?" Because the last words of my Saviour were, "Go and get people born again." I want to grant His request. I want to give Him that which He asks me to give Him. So I must needs be about the Father's business.

We hasten on down to Luke. The last thing Luke records Jesus saying was this:

> "And, behold, I send the promise of my Father upon you: but tarry ye in Jerusalem, until ye be endued with power from on high."--Luke 24:49.

Luke, the great physician, said, "What shall I tell the people? What is the last thing You want me to record in my book?" Jesus said, "Tell them to get the power of the Holy Ghost of God. Tell them to be anointed from Heaven. Tell them to tarry in Jerusalem until power comes so sinners can be born into My family."

We hasten to say what John records. The last words John recorded about Jesus were, "Follow me."

Well, you say, "Preacher, I know now that soul winning is not the important thing because the last words Jesus said in John were, 'Follow me.'" I want to call your attention to the words that Jesus spoke to people when He said, "Follow me," when He said to those fishermen that day, "Follow me. I will make you fishers of men." Ah! You can't follow Jesus without getting folks saved. You just can't follow Him without having a burning heart and a burning soul for sinners headed for Hell, to get born of the Spirit of God.

His first words were concerning salvation; His last words were concerning salvation.

Woodrow Wilson quoted John 3:16 when he died. Daniel Webster said, "Amen! Amen!" Through these years I have seen many, many people die. One little lady in Texas began to sing as she crossed the Jordan, and she said, "I am longing for the coming of the snow white angel band!" She reached out her old eighty-year-old hand to her husband, gripped it, and said, "Sweetheart, I am going to Heaven! The angels are coming to get me!" I remember that dear man in the hospital one night who said, "Keep preaching the Bible, Brother Jack," and bowed his head, folded his hands, and slipped across into the other world. Last words are tremendously important.

Let us hasten on. Not only were Jesus' last words important, not only were His first words important but

His Next Words Are Important

Now we know what He said first in the Bible, in Matthew, in Mark, Luke and John. We know what He said last in the Bible, in Matthew, Mark, Luke and John. But He hasn't spoken through these years. Today we have not heard the audible voice of Jesus speak. What will be the next words of Jesus Christ? I am not sure what they will be, but I Thessalonians, chapter 4, verse 16, says:

> "For the Lord himself shall descend from heaven with a shout."

When Jesus comes back, He will come with a shout. I don't know what He will say. Maybe it will be, "Hallelujah!" Maybe He will say, "Glory to God!" Maybe we will hear Him say, "Come forth!" I don't know what He will say, but the next time we hear the voice of Jesus it will be a shout. And I think He is going to say, "Come forth!"

You recall in the eleventh chapter of John that Mary and Martha came to Jesus and said, "Our brother is sick." Jesus tarried that day. They came back and said, "If you hadn't tarried, our brother would not be dead. But he is dead now." After he had been dead four days and his body was already stinking, Jesus came. What did He say? "Lazarus, come forth!" And Lazarus came forth. Bound, and they unbound him, and let him go and he lived again.

A little boy said, "Mamma, do you know why Jesus said, 'Lazarus, come forth?'"

Mamma said, "No, Johnny."

Johnny said, "He said 'Lazarus, come forth' because if He hadn't called Lazarus' name, everybody in the grave would have come forth all at one time."

There will be a day when Jesus shall come from Heaven and He will say, "Come forth!" He will come with a shout. Then when He does come, He will say to those who have been saved, born again, and have lived for Him, "Well done, thou good and faithful servant."

I don't have many degrees from colleges, though I have some. I have been to college and seminary. I am on the co-operating board and a trustee in a number of universities. But I am not a whole lot worried about that. The D. D. doesn't impress me very much. The M. D. never impresses me very much, in spite of Dr. Rollins who did such a good job in getting my little girl here! I heard a preacher say one time that the M. D. and D. D. and LL. D. stand for

Mairsey Dotes and
Doesy Dotes and
Little Lambsy Divy,

but I am not sure about that! I am not too much concerned about getting the big degrees, but I want the W. D. I want Jesus to be able to write my name in Heaven, Jack Hyles, W. D. I want to hear Jesus say, "Well done! Well done!" when He comes. The Bible says when the great Antichrist, the man of sin, is revealed, Jesus shall come from Heaven and shall destroy him and set up His kingdom. How is He going to do it? Second Thessalonians, chapter 2, verse 8 says "with the spirit of his mouth," the Word of God. Jesus shall speak, nations shall crumble, and He shall rule over all the earth.

Then in Revelation 19, verses 11 through 14, when Jesus comes in clouds of glory and all the holy angels and all the saints with Him, and He comes Himself in glory, the great

Saviour coming back again, the Bible says, "What is His name?" Somebody says, "No one knows His name." And somebody else says, "Here is His name. His name is called the Word of God." Thank God for the words of Jesus!

"Suffer little children and forbid them not....In my Father's house are many mansions....Let not your heart be troubled...My peace I give unto you....I will not leave you comfortless....Come unto me, all ye that labour and are heavy laden....Him that cometh unto me, I will in no wise cast out." Think of the wonderful words of Jesus.

We have seen His first words, we have seen His last words, we have seen His next words; what are His

Present Words?

His present words are, Salvation is opened to all men. His present word is, You may be saved. You don't have to go to Hell. You can go to Heaven. You can be born again. His present words are words of hope and victory and salvation and a home in Heaven free to all who will believe it.

What are His present words? "Whosoever shall call upon the name of the Lord shall be saved." What are His present words? "Him that cometh unto me, I will in no wise cast out." What are His present words? "As many as received him, to them gave he power to become the sons of God, even to them that believe on his name." What are His present words? "Whosoever believeth on him shall not perish, but have everlasting life."

We have seen His first words, His last words, His next words, His present words. I want to say this.

Yesterday we celebrated something big at our house. Our birthdays are always important, tremendously important. We make a big to-do about birthdays. Yesterday was Becky's eighth birthday. We carried her down town and shopped awhile, and she got some gifts and got her birthday cake, and we sang "Happy Birthday" and lit the candles, of course, and all that goes with it. Then I said to Becky yesterday: "Becky, how would you like to do something you have never done before?"

She said, "What, Daddy?"

"How would you like to go visiting with Daddy today? We will go out together and try to win somebody to Jesus together."

"Oh," she said, "I would like to do that."

So we got in the car, drove by the church, got some prospect cards. She was my secretary; she took care of the prospect cards. We prayed in the car, we prayed for God to give us somebody to come to Christ. We went visiting. Soon we went into a home and there was a man alone.

I said, "Where is your wife?"

He said, "She is in St. Marcus Hospital."

I said, "Oh, sure enough?"

He said, "We have a new baby girl."

I said, "Well, we can talk business here! It so happens that my wife is also in St. Marcus Hospital, and we have a bigger baby girl than you have!"

We talked. After awhile I said to him, "Why is my little girl better than your little girl?"

Of course he implied that she wasn't better than his little girl.

I asked him then this question, "Well, then, if my little girl is no better than yours, why does my little girl have the opportunity of having a Christian father and your little girl does not have that opportunity?"

That struck home. To make a long story short, it wasn't long until we fell on our knees in the room, and the little baby had a Christian daddy. He is here this morning; he is going to come down in a minute and let me tell you that he has been saved.

So last night, before leaving for the Mission, I got Becky and hugged her and told her how happy I was to be her father. She said, "You are the best daddy in all the world." Of course I knew that already! I said, "You are the sweetest little eight-year-old girl that ever lived." And we made love to each other. She had gotten a new dress from me, a new dress from David (of course I helped him on it financially), a little toy from me, Brother Jim and Dorothy had given her some houseshoes, and a lovely cake, and a wonderful day. I said, "Becky, what did you enjoy best about today?"

Without stopping to think a minute she passed up the dress, the little ping pong set, the houseshoes and the cake, and she got real serious and said, "Daddy, the thing I enjoyed the most was when me and you won that man to Jesus this afternoon."

That is what Jesus came for. Those are His words to you. If you will believe in Him, He will save you. If you will come to Christ, you can have Heaven. He will give you, free of charge, eternal life and you can live forever in Heaven. You say, "How may I get it?" Simply by trusting in Him and His work on Calvary as your hope for Heaven.

We have seen His last words, His first words, His next words, His present words; then may I say that the last words that He ever said in the Bible were the words in Revelation 22: "Surely I come quickly." Dear Jesus, You have said in Matthew and in Mark, "Go." You said in Luke, "Tarry to be endued with power." You have said in John to follow You and You would make us fishers of men. Now Jesus, of all these things, what is the

Most Important Thing You Want to Leave?

We are almost through the Bible, Jesus. We are almost finished--over here in the last book, dear Jesus, and we are down to the last chapter, the last few verses. Dear Jesus, we want You to tell us now what is the thing that You want people to know. What is the last thing You want to say? Tell us quickly: What can we put in the last verses in the Bible?

Jesus said, "Tell the people, Surely I come quickly."

So I repeat to you this morning, my precious friends, Jesus Christ is going to come. It may be today. It may be tomorrow. It may be Tuesday. It may be Wednesday. I do not know, but one thing I do know, that is,

> **Some golden daybreak Jesus will come;**
> **Some golden daybreak, battles all won,**
> **He'll shout the victory, break through the blue,**
> **Some golden daybreak, for me, for you.**

If you do not know Him before He comes, I beg you, by faith receive Him as your Saviour and have eternal life as your possession.

I take you for a minute inside a little treasured place in my own heart and share with you an experience that to me ranks among the greatest experiences of my life. I had never carried my boy baby to a service before to visit while I preached. Last night when I started to the Union Gospel Mission and to enjoy good fellowship with dear friends there, I turned to David and said, "David, how would you like to go tonight and hear Daddy preach?"

He jumped two feet in the air and said, "Okay! Can Becky go with me?"

"No, you have got to sit by yourself and be a good boy for an hour."

Now that's a big order for my boy! So he took off his blue jeans, "T" shirt, got on some other clothes, got his coat and his cap, got in the car, and we drove down to the Mission. He heard me preach on "The Three Appearances of Nicodemus in the Bible." He sat frozen looking at me. As we left the service he said, "Daddy, that's one of the best churches I have ever been to"--the Rescue Mission. He enjoyed the message. David is a little tyke, not quite six. I often talked to David about salvation. About once a week he and I have a private little talk about salvation. I talked to him going home, but this time we didn't mention a thing about salvation. I just made love to him a little bit. That is what every mother and daddy should do.

We drove home and I got something to carry to the hospital to Mrs. Hyles for that baby. They didn't have anything there big enough to fit her! So I kissed David goodnight, and Becky and Linda, and went on to the hospital. David went to bed.

When I came in about 10:40 the light was on. My mother, who is staying with us, said, "Son, David has been crying. He came in and said, 'Mam Maw, I want to be saved.'" Some of you are wondering why a little boy not quite six could know how to be saved. If you had dealt with your little boy as many times as I have dealt with mine, and taught him how to get saved, you would understand. When he was five days old, and a week old, and ten days old we told him, and almost every week for almost six years we have told him salvation's plan from Adam in the Garden of Eden to Heaven.

I carried him down stairs--just me and him--a men's meeting. We had a little talk. I have never seen a boy that young under conviction like he was. He looked at me just like he would look at a businessman.

"I want to get saved," and he started crying. I told him how again. We knelt and prayed. After we got through praying, I said, "David, what do you want to say now?"

He started grinning. Becky, when she got saved, had a wonderful experience. But David had a tremendous burden lifted, and he said, "Now, only ones ain't saved in our family is Linda Lou and Cindy." He had come to Christ. And I had the blessed experience.

He went in and woke up Becky. She rejoiced and led us in prayer, because God had saved David. We called Mother on the phone at the hospital and told her about it. We called Jim, and David told Jim about it. He said, "I want to call everybody! Can I call Texas and tell them about it?"

When Becky prayed she said, "Dear Jesus, thank You that now all of us will meet You in the air when You come."

You can be saved the same way. The last words that Jesus gave were, "Surely I come quickly." If He came right now, Becky and David would rise over here. My mother is at Munster today preparing for Mrs. Hyles' return--she would rise over there. And my wife in the hospital would rise from there. (By the way, Brother Jim, you would have to finish the sermon, because I would rise too, to meet the Lord in the air!)

Why do I know that? Because I have been born again. I am saved.

Redeemed--how I love to proclaim it!
Redeemed by the blood of the Lamb.
Redeemed through His infinite mercy,
His child, and forever, I am.

Gone, gone, gone, gone!
Yes, my sins are gone.
Now my soul is free, and in my
my heart's a song;
Buried in the deepest sea,
Yes, that's good enough for me;
I shall live eternally,
Praise God! My sins are gone!

Will you bow your heads for prayer. While heads are bowed, how many of you can say with me, "Preacher, if Jesus' last words happened today, if He did come right now, I too would rise to meet Him. I am His child. I have been saved. I know it." Will you lift your hand up high as a testimony? God bless you! You may put your hands down.

I wonder how many would say with me, "Brother Preacher, I do not know I am saved. I do not know that if Jesus came this morning, I would meet Him in the air. But I would like to know. I want to be saved. I want to go to Heaven. Would you pray for me, that I might be saved?" If so, will you lift your hand, all over this great crowd? God bless you, and you, and you. Oh, yes, there are many. God bless you, young lady at the front. Yes, dear man, I see you under the balcony to the left.

With heads bowed and eyes closed, listen carefully. Would you do right here where you are what my boy did last night? Would you say this to God, "O God, have mercy on me, a sinner, and save me now. I do now receive Jesus as my Saviour, and trust Him to take me to Heaven when I die." Jesus said, "Him that cometh to me, I will in no wise cast out."

We are going to stand and sing, and when we do, I am going to ask every one of you who raised your hand to leave your seat, come to the nearest aisle, out of the balcony, and come to this altar and pray, "Jesus, I come." He said He would in no wise cast you out. Will you come to Him?

PRAYER: Dear Father, help, we pray, each of these who have lifted their hands and others who did not to come on the first stanza and make their decision for Jesus Christ, trusting You as their Saviour. Help them, dear Lord, on the first note, the first word, to make this step for Christ. In Jesus' name, Amen.